A Gift of Sacred Guidance / Illuminating the Path for the Children of the One

A Gift of Sacred Guidance / Illuminating the Path for the Children of the One

AGANRIUS

FLEETING GLIMPSES LLC
FREDERICKSBURG

Contents

Part II. YOU ARE A CREATOR

Part III. DIVERSITY

Part IV. JUDGEMENT AND JUSTICE

Part V. FREEDOM

Part VI. REVERANCE FOR LIFE

Part VII. LIVING IN THE MOMENT

Part VIII. TURNING WITHIN

Part IX. SPIRITUAL ATTRIBUTES

Part X. THE SPIRITUAL

Part XI. DEATH AND REINCARNATION

Part XII. PATHWAYS TO GOD

Part XIII. THE WAY OF THE PILGRIM

Part XIV. THE END OF DUALITY

Part XV. CONSCIOUS EVOLUTION

Part XVI. THE LIGHT

Introduction

THIS BOOK IS DEDICATED TO

THOSE WHO CAN HEAR *What it is saying*

WITH THE SINCEREST WISH IT MAY CONFIRM

THEIR INNERMOST THOUGHTS AND FEELINGS

The Front Cover - Tree of Life

The Front Cover

The Tree of Life represents the interconnectedness of everything in the universe.
The Tree of Life serves as a worshiping point. A source of Sacred Knowledge.
The Tree of Life naturally grows upwards and outwards. This is symbolic of how a person develops...growing stronger and wiser over each of their lifetimes.
The Tree of Life symbolizes a person's personal growth into a unique human being as each different life experience shapes them into who they are meant to become.
The Tree of Life symbolizes immortality. Even as the tree grows old, it creates seeds that carry its Sacred Essence...as is Gods' Plan with us.

Preface

PREFACE

The TRUE story of creation is born ANEW each day within the hearts of man.

It has NEVER been captured by either chisel, plume or pen, for it is never complete, but ongoing and Eternal.

It is never literal but is in constant change and motion as is the CREATOR, ITSELF.

IT is always vital, fresh and daring, for IT has NO limits or bounds.

ITS true essence is FREEDOM and LOVE, though IT manifests through law and order.

It is impossible to restrain or limit IT by the rules and commandments of man.

The CREATOR is eternally revealing ITSELF to any who have eyes to see, and IT is far different from the God YOU have created in your OWN image and likeness.

IT is the ONE that will deliver you from your "sins" and the chaos YOU have created.

You are well known, indeed, and you are deeply loved, for you and the CREATOR are ONE. You are FREE to ABIDE within ITS great Peace and Love – it is YOUR choice.*

*Note – the word IT is used to emphasize that the Creator (God) is SPIRIT and HAS no gender.

Ritas' Recollection

In 2005 I met this "Scribe" and his wife while teaching an Iridology class in Kerrville TX. We quickly became companions in our similar spiritual beliefs and metaphysical concepts.

We agreed to meet weekly, and it was during these discussions that he reported that his daily journaling had changed, and that a different energy/voice came through..."I've been waiting a long time for this kind of transmission" he said; "this is different than my daily inspirational journaling...when I asked who are you the answer was 'We are a group of many'."

Each new reading he received, became a deep discussion about our Spirit having a human experience in the daily pilgrimage.

As I became familiar with his style of writing, my intellect expanded into an awareness of how connected we all are and that nothing happens by accident.

The transmissions continually say "All IS ONE" and "GOD IS ALL THAT IS" and "GO IN GREAT PEACE AND LOVE".

Used as a daily meditation, these thought provoking concepts are for the metaphysical student striving for a higher understanding and contemplation of the Souls journey. The Scribes intentions were that this material be distributed freely and for him to remain anonymous.

Rita Bernadette

Chapters

SUBJECT CATEGORIES:

PART II
CREATION

1. THE DICTATION BEGINS

I await each morning with you with eagerness, for there is so much that I wish to relate to you.

While it seems to you that these are trying times, you are actually experiencing one of the most exciting periods of Spiritual growth ever. The world is changing very, very rapidly and there is so much more happening than you have any idea. It is a very great honor to be here at this time and the work to be done is overwhelming.

Each one has an important part to play in this event and no one else can do it in your manner. Please be aware that every day counts, and it may seem to you that nothing is happening. It IS occurring and at great speed. Your response to every issue and encounter is of the utmost importance. Ponder the results of each comment or suggestion you make, for the meanings reach far deeper than you are aware. Never lose sight of the fact that you are all indeed brothers and that your present choices affect many others. Live with the idea that whatever you do or say, you are doing to YOURSELF. It is LITERALLY true. Keep your eyes and ears open for the seemingly unimportant events, for they are deeper and contain more than would seem. Know that all is well, all is in balance and know that you have nothing to fear. Remain true to your principles and give any encouragement you can offer to those around you. This is not a time for pessimism, but for watchful expectation. You may be called upon for assistance. Be prepared to offer what you have to give.

May I ask the source?

The Response: IT is much nearer than you think. IT is always with you and you know IT well. You call IT by many names, but it is all ONE.

2. THE LESSONS YOU RECEIVE

The lessons you receive are not only colored by the filter of your PERCEPTION but they are also formed from your own knowledge and understanding.

It is actually not information which comes to you from an OUTSIDE source as you believe but is selected by us from that which you already possess and know SUBCONSCIOUSLY.

It is for this reason that it often seems so familiar to you, for IT IS.

This is, perhaps, a far different concept from that which is generally held and understood. You are most definitely guided, but in ways you do not always understand.

We are bringing to your awareness who you actually ARE, but this by no means reduces our significance in your development. The experiences of your daily lives add to the accumulated awareness of your Spiritual understanding and are far more Spiritual in nature than you yet believe.

You do not understand what you are doing when you attempt to JUDGE another, for this judgment of Spiritual REALITY is being made from a PHYSICAL point of view. When you finally awaken to the reality of your being, you will awaken to another world.

That world is approaching ever so swiftly. Do not falter along the way but go forth in God's Great Peace and Love. Move on into the LIGHT.

3. THE ONE

THE ONE is the God of Peace and Love. ITS existence is REALITY and ITS words are TRUE.

IT is speaking to those who can hear and understand what IT is saying, and these words will ring out loud and clear. They have been TRUE all along, but the appeal of the physical world has been too strong and has overridden the call for peace. The lures of power and wealth have brought your world to an impasse and the hopelessness of your situation is opening the eyes of many who are becoming aware of the TRUTH, and they will recognize it soon when it is put into words. Open yourselves to the wisdom, which is your BIRTHRIGHT and CLAIM your inheritance, for it is of great value. You are all loved and guided but you must accept it and apply it in your daily lives. It was not God who brought you into your current situation, but YOU, yourselves.

You have the capacity to completely change your direction into one of peace and love, but you must desire this ABOVE all things. You are truly creators, and you WILL experience that which you create. Your deepest desire, when held constantly in mind, WILL bring into manifestation that which you are creating mentally. This may be either positive or otherwise.

It is YOU who selects your experiences and it is of no avail to simply bemoan the results. You can have and experience the life that appears to be so evasive by concentrating your full attention in this direction. You can also, to a remarkable extent, fill in the details. This requires, first of all, the DECISION to do so and the discipline to control your thinking. Belief and patience are also necessary. Your thoughts are literally two-edged swords, that can cut in either direction.

4. IT

IT is the fountainhead of all being. Nothing exists apart from IT. IT is all sacred. IT is all holy....IT is eternally active, creating and expanding.

Man is incapable of limiting IT by his refusal to accept ITS' universality.

It is futile to attempt to move against ITS currents, for they are all-inclusive. You will become all you are capable of becoming by flowing in Harmony with IT. And all will eventually be carried along in ITS stream and return to its destiny – its SOURCE.

It matters not if you believe IT at this point, for the day of your awakening is drawing ever nearer. All the arbitrary divisions of man will eventually melt away in the warmth of ITS love.

IT is all ONE. IT is ALL THAT IS.

You will, indeed, have no other gods before IT. You are actually already there, but you are still asleep and do not recognize IT. You are now living in the period of the great awakening as foretold by so many mystics and prophets. It is occurring now.

IT is in-the-midst of you and many will be the wonders that you will see.

Many ARE now beginning to see through the illusion which has divided man from his brother and separated him from his God, for you are SPIRITUAL beings and you are ETERNAL.

You are FREE at any time to enter into the REALITY of your being. Go forth in God's Great Peace and Love. ALL IS ONE.

5. ON OBSERVING NATURE

Your inner Truths and Reality will always ultimately form your world.

This, you have heard many times, though you are unaware of how quickly it is approaching. Where there is a marked difference between the two, the manifestations may not appear to be so obvious.

It may seem to be approaching very slowly, and yet the outer changes are overwhelming. It is still difficult to see beyond the APPARENT confusion of today's world, for the appearance of anything positive still seems remote.

It would be most helpful at this time to observe nature as much as you can.

Although it too is changing, the Creative Forces are still more easily observed...thus making it much easier to RELATE to Creation.

The more enduring aspects of nature help to provide a sense of stability at a time when it is so desperately needed.

Do not allow yourselves to become caught up in the drama of the PLAY. Recognize it for what it is but continue to follow your OWN path.

You are ALWAYS being guided. Move ahead in Peace.

6. THE CREATIVE FORCES

It is not without a DEEPER understanding of the nature of the Creative Forces that you will be able to grasp the inner meanings of your experiences.

All of life is a REFLECTION of the Mind of God. IT is INFINITE in ITS scope and IT conceives on every level of existence and consciousness.

We have given you some brief examples of the interweaving of REALITY which exists on countless levels and dimensions. The ripples which are generated by the SLIGHTEST change at any point eventually extend to and are felt entirely throughout Creation. It is not within the realm of possibility to alter or to inhibit any aspect of ITS FUNCTIONING.

Change occurs when NEW creative thoughts are introduced into this "system", for they WILL make their journey throughout Creation. Everything that exists or ever shall exist begins as a THOUGHT in the mind of ALL THAT IS. This process is further extended as that which is created also begins to create.

This could perhaps give a better understanding of the "big bang" theory. That which is created is Eternal, though IT immediately begins to CHANGE as IT extends ITSELF. Each manifestation and experience then alters the entire picture to some degree. This is all accomplished in complete FREEDOM, for there ARE no restrictions or limitations. As we have already said, it is not possible to make a judgment in any sense, for all is in constant change and growth.

There IS no duality, IT is all ultimately ONE. ITS reality is so vast, that IT is truly inconceivable to the human mind. It could appear, then, that man's situation is virtually out of his hands, but this is far from true. Man's immediate surroundings are intensely affected by HIS contributions to the process.

The results of your creations and the understanding you will gain will further alter the total outcome. It would seem, though, that anything which might be thought to be a personal relationship with God would be impossible, but this is not SO. God extends ITSELF at every point in the process and is eternally in "direct contact" with ITS offspring. Each being is always a witness to Creation, each is equal in the overall scheme of things and each is a vital ASPECT of ALL THAT IS. Each is part of GOD. Each, a creator. And each is ETERNAL.

All is ONE. May your thoughts be in complete harmony with your deepest desires, for they WILL create what you actually "request".

7. THE WORLD IS AN IDEA

It is the intelligence and energy of ALL THAT IS which conceives and drives the universe. It was well said that the world is an idea in the mind of GOD, for it is SO.

IT is both the creative URGE ITSELF, as well as ITS SOURCE – IT is God, as IT manifests ITS deepest longings and desires.

Creativity, as we have said, is man's deepest connection with ALL THAT IS. It is innate within him, for he carries the Essence of the memory of Creation recorded upon every atom and molecule of his being.

Creativity and the learning experiences which result, then become the driving force of man as well. There were none who were denied this impulse – it was granted to all.

True creativity cannot be learned – it is already there and can only be recognized. To allow its energy to flow freely through you – through your entire being, is the beginning of a true transformation from a life of ACQUIRING to a life of BEING.

By carefully watching and studying your inner longings and desires, you will come to see and to understand your CREATOR within. When this is approached through love, there is no greater contact with the Source. If you dwell on the SURFACE of your consciousness, you will never become aware of the vast treasure which lies buried beneath. Where your treasure is, there will your heart be also.

8. MAKE YOUR EYE SINGLE

And the material world and all that is found therein emerges continually from the formless.

ITS creation is ongoing and without pause – there are no seams to be found. It is the product of the MOMENT – time plays no part in it.

The Creator is to be found in EVERY aspect of ITS Creation, and YOU are never apart from IT. The eye cannot behold ITSELF but must be observed by the eyes of another.

You are, then, never apart from God nor out of ITS sight. It is only the blind who seek God elsewhere, for they do not know for what they are seeking.

The Eye of God beholds ITS own LIGHT in ALL of Creation, for there IS no darkness. God is therefore to be seen in ALL THAT IS – nothing else is there. You need only make your eye single and you will recognize only THE ONE.

IT IS ALL THAT IS.

9. MAKE YOUR EYES SINGLE

Those who earnestly strive to make their eyes single will prevail and all else will completely dissolve with their efforts, for they are answering the CALL of the ONE.

A HOUSE DIVIDED AGAINST ITSELF CANNOT STAND...and so it is with the present world.

It is by no means a psychotic dream of some who are incapable of participating in society, but rather, a movement which will bring about a New World.

The leaders of the nation's speak loudly of FREEDOM as they continue to control and restrict their people. True freedom CAN NOT be established by rules and restrictions but can only flourish when EACH is fulfilling his life purpose.

The lust for money and power ALWAYS results in the enslavement of the many by the few. There are now many who are seeing ANOTHER way.

Lip service is of no more value than are eyes which do not see REALITY.

Fear not the noise and clamor of the outside world, it is the result of the oncoming change. We remind you that TRUE change can ONLY come from WITHIN and the REAL world is also to be found only WITHIN.

All else is but illusion.

10. CREATION AS AN EXTENSION OF GOD

The true story of Creation is far more complete, and vast than that as suggested in scripture.

As you have been given, the first Creation was that which occurred in the MIND of GOD. EVERYTHING CONCEIVABLE – EVERY POSSIBILITY was formed in this act. NOTHING whatsoever EXISTS which did not find its origin in this source.

Its essential reality was formed in the realm of ideas and the patterns for "material" forms and objects appeared as matrices of energetic patterns which are indestructible. They can only be changed by thought. You might think of the material of matter or the alphabet of Creation as "cosmic soup".

ITS' manifestation as REALITY is, in a sense, the second Creation and is ongoing and eternal. IT was extended from the BEING of the God Force, ITSELF. IT IS GOD – IT IS ALL THAT IS and IT continues to create from this level also.

What you think of as SOULS are also energetic fields – Extensions of God.

They were created at once and are also Eternal and Sacred. There is NO evolution as now understood, for everything that exists is a UNIQUE Creation. The second Creation is the story of GOD experiencing ITSELF and ITS ideas and concepts THROUGH these extensions of ITSELF. Every conceivable possibility, every situation, every thought is, in effect, a Divine Creation. The stage for this story is INFINITY. There are NO limits. GOD IS ALL THAT IS. ALL IS ONE. You, also, are an important part of this story, for you, too, are deeply involved in it.

11. CREATION

THE ONE is divisible only by ITSELF and this simple statement tells the story of Creation.

Within ITS ancient dreams, IT conceived EVERY possibility, and each became so. Each glowed with Creative Energy and each became vital and moved on ITS own.

Everything then came into EXISTENCE as a DREAM in the realm of the mind.

IT became INFINITE when IT too, began to express ITSELF in whatever way IT could most benefit, and the LIVING universe came into being and CONTINUES to form and to expand into Eternity.

All IS ALIVE, ALL IS ONE, but ONE divided by ONE remains ONE.

Nothing EXISTS apart from IT or ever will.

Each possibility has been included and will be experienced as we grow TOGETHER. We are ETERNAL and we are ONE. Our existence is the ultimate adventure, for we can only experience, grow and learn. That which unites us is LOVE for it is the BOND of unity. Thus, ALL came into being and we began our Eternal adventure.

Rejoice in this, for ALL IS SACRED, ALL IS TRUE, and ALL IS ONE.

In the beginning
God created the heavens and the earth.
Judaism

12. I AM WITH YOU

I am with you always. My strength is your strength, my wish is YOUR desire and my days are your lifetimes.

I have neither departed from your side nor left you alone and lost on your way. My love enfolds you and embraces you as does the warmth of the sun in spring. You are mine.

Your feet have trod my paths and your hands have formed that which I ached to see and to experience THROUGH you.

You did not fall or depart from my ways, for I am always there. Your most SECRET thought was already MINE...and I rejoice in it.

My ways are YOUR ways and you could not depart from them, even should you so desire. We are ONE, though you know it not. We have always been and shall always be. We are creating this story together, for it is yours as well as mine.

Thus, it has always been. I sought to find if you would forget me, but you have not and my soul sings for joy. Our story is without beginning and is endless.

Together, there is nothing we will not experience, and I created your BODIES to enable me to express myself in ways I could never do alone. You are blessed beyond your greatest imagination – as am I. This then, is our story. This is the book we are writing together on the pages of Eternity.

13. IT GIVES ME GREAT JOY

It gives me great joy when I am able to communicate with my children. I am always with you. I am always accessible as I INTENDED to be.

I am not, nor have I ever been, remote and separated. I have never been apart from you. I am Love, Life and Creativity.

I am the master craftsman and I rejoice in my creativity, for all was conceived with my deepest love and care.

I create NOTHING which is unworthy or does not have its place. I do not demand of you that which you cannot achieve. The simplicity of Creation evades you and your efforts sometimes take you far from me.

You are assigning to me those ideas which frighten you the most, but I am NOT the spirit of anger and wrath, or of punishment and revenge. I require no priest-craft to protect my name or to appease me with flattery and sacrifices.

You are attempting to place another before me, but there IS none. You have only to listen to the words I speak silently within to know my TRUTH. If they speak of other than Love and Creativity, they are not mine, but your OWN.

I am calling you to awaken from YOUR world of illusion and to learn WHO you are.

For you have forgotten.

I AM ALL THAT IS. There IS only ONE. Enter in Great Peace and Love.

14. YOUR CREATOR

Your complete acceptance of each brother – just as he is, is best approached by seeking the Creator WITHIN you. For IT is ALWAYS present.

This approach will simultaneously broaden your understanding of ALL THAT IS.

The Creator expresses ITSELF through DIVERSITY which is found in EVERY aspect of Creation – conformity is RESTRICTIVE.

As we have so often stated, your Creator is infinitely more vast than you can even BEGIN to comprehend, and Creation extends FAR beyond your range of understanding. Man cannot limit that which is INFINITE. You have created a god which pales beside THE ONE.

As a result, you have greatly restricted the range of your lives and you have suffered for it. It is by no means more spiritual to attempt to define God simply according to the accounts found in scripture.

That which was portrayed therein was the deity as seen through THEIR eyes and filtered through THEIR understanding. The Creator, and Creation, is ongoing and EVERYTHING is alive...extending ITSELF into Infinity.

This understanding must be approached with great humility. It is sufficient to see EVERYTHING as part of ALL THAT IS – as an ASPECT of Creation. For ALL IS indeed ONE. Only in this LIGHT can you go your way in God's Great Peace and Love, for you, too are unique, but you simply refuse to accept it.

15. THE FOUNTAINHEAD

The Source of ALL BEING is to be found and is active within YOU.

IT is the same Source from which universes spring forth.

IT is not limited to a remote place in outer space which must be reached through advanced technology but resides within every living cell of your body.

You are not, nor have you ever been apart from the Creator – it is not possible.

It is pointless to seek IT within another while ignoring THE ONE which dwells WITHIN.

The term "the God of your heart" conveys a Truth few comprehend. There IS no other to grant you grace or forgiveness. There is no better guidance to be found.

The Fountainhead of Wisdom and Truth is very, very near, indeed. There is no other who knows you better or who loves you more deeply.

ALL IS ONE. There is no room for duality. GOD IS ALL THAT IS. Why do you attempt to place another before IT?

PART III
YOU ARE A CREATOR

TOPICS

16. ALLOWING CREATIVITY

It is characteristic of those who are truly creative to ALLOW it to come to them. Nothing really worthwhile can be accomplished by force.

Force is always the mark of the immature, but the REAL SECRET is to learn to prepare yourself to RECEIVE that which you are creating, for it will come to you from your highest level.

These are the creations which are truly inspired, and they are clearly transmitted to those who come-into-contact with them. The inner sources for such inspirations are many – though they are all connected with your own Spiritual being.

Your 'contacts' are far more extensive than you are aware and cover subjects and areas of ability of which you have never consciously dreamed. It would truly be worth your effort to carefully study your more random thoughts, for you are constantly being given clues from your over-self, and it is vast indeed.

If an unusual idea appears in your mind, it is often in some way connected with a latent ability you possess. A more careful study along these lines would be much like going through the card files of a library. Your current approach is mostly a matter of scratching in the dark, for you have no idea for what you are searching.

So much of your effort is lost by your continually repeating the same "messages", as they have usually been long since exhausted and have nothing more to offer. A real study of your own mind would be highly rewarding, for it would be similar to receiving the key to a private library which was collected especially for YOU – and such it is. There are so many ways in which you can extend your own consciousness thereby extending your own BORDERS far beyond that which you have accepted. For each of you, your inner knowledge exceeds this by far.

17. THERE IS A RIVER

The stream of CONSCIOUS AWARENESS is like unto a river which flows eternally from the mind of the Creator into INFINITY.

It is the stream in which God projects ITSELF into each soul.

It is a connecting link which permits IT to experience ITS own Creations. This stream is Sacred, and It is Eternal.

EACH soul is far more than a spark – IT is an ASPECT of THE ONE.

EVERYTHING IS ALIVE and Everything is conscious in its own way, for it is all a projection from the mind of God. ALL is indeed, one.

The divisions which man beholds are illusion – they do not exist as man perceives them. It is the concept of UNITY which will unite THE CHILDREN OF THE ONE and usher in a new age of Peace and Understanding.

We are, indeed, all ONE – all Aspects of God – Sacred, Eternal, ever expanding, growing and creating. How different, then, is life when beheld in this Light.

Each experience is always in the moment – the Eternal Now, whatever it may be. To move along in harmony with IT is to accept IT as ALL THAT IS. Then you will experience life in its fullness – in its completeness.

Open yourself to IT and go forth in God's Great Peace and Love. ALL IS ONE.

18. YOUR ROLE AS A CREATOR

You are in greater control of your own life than you are yet aware, and your abilities as a creator reach far beyond your understanding.

It is very important for you to realize the nature of this gift, to take responsibility for it and to use it wisely and to its greatest advantage. It is for this reason that we have been REPEATING many things.

The true nature of your being is SPIRITUAL.

The physical world is NOT your home, but a STAGE where you come to play out roles you have selected to enable you to experience the lessons you need to learn at this point. It can be a beautiful world, indeed, and the physical and material attractions are often very appealing. Though many of the lessons can be bitter and heartbreaking.

It is very easy to forget that this is not your REAL life, but only a ROLE. For you will soon move into ANOTHER completely new experience. It becomes so much easier when you are aware of the true meaning of life and view it from this point, for you will realize that life is truly ETERNAL and that you are safe and loved. You are never alone and forgotten in a hostile environment. You have the ability to REDIRECT your life whenever you so desire. You must, however, deeply DESIRE to do so and to KNOW that you are a creator. You must always remember that you WILL experience the results of your creations and it is in this manner that your "lesson" becomes complete. You are now and will always remain part of God – of ALL THAT IS – who experiences the totality of ITS Creation THROUGH you. ALL IS ONE, all is in Divine order and you are empowered to EXTEND Creation as you desire. The possibilities are endless, they are all TRUE and they change not only your OWN experience but ALL THAT IS.

19. STRIVE NOT TO BE DIFFERENT

Many of you are now seeking your pathway – but there are MANY paths. Your call is to live your OWN truth, whatever it may be.

No rules can point it out, for the path is YOURS only. Thus, it is pointless to strive to be different, for THAT you are already.

You need only to recognize your own inner truth and to accept it as your MISSION in life. Oddly enough, though many of you desire to be different, you find it difficult to accept your TRUE uniqueness as a soul.

Your place HAS been prepared for you and you already possess the abilities which will make it yours. Your response can be as complex or as simple as you choose to make it.

The simple path is often far more amazing in its effectiveness than are the convoluted trails of complexity which all too often become confused and lost.

You have been granted the ability to CREATE your own life story, but you must begin now, for there is no OTHER possibility. It is YOU who must act. There IS no tomorrow. Only NOW.

Seize the moment. It is ALL THAT IS.

20. INSPIRATION...THE GUIDING LIGHT

Inspiration is the guiding light which leads to Creativity. It is the gift of God to those who will follow its beam in any Creative endeavor.

Inspiration, like Creativity itself, has no limits and its power has led men everywhere through the darkness into the most brilliant of activities. Inspiration has no favorite other than a willingness of one to open oneself to its leadership. It is usually highly spontaneous and can shine forth at any time. Inspiration itself, is very modest and makes no claims to greatness or fame, though its results become a gift to all of mankind. Since it is a gift, it is not easy to cultivate or attract other than by becoming truly conscious and living in the MOMENT.

Its light attracts those who are truly searching for a particular pathway which is hidden by the darkness of UNKNOWING. Its appearance is very similar to that of the inner voice – it can easily become overshadowed by the clamor of the outside world and lost to an individual who was seeking.

Fortunately, it remains accessible to others through the collective consciousness. This has been observed many times by the simultaneous appearance of a new idea or invention in widely separated areas of the world. Similar thoughts are mutually attracted to form impulses of GREATER magnitude which are then able to direct the course of man. Your thoughts contribute to the development of your civilization and touch others far removed from you and who have no conscious awareness of your existence. You are by no means insignificant in the scheme of things, for ALL IS ONE and ALL THAT IS would be incomplete WITHOUT you. Your every thought is deeply involved in Creation. Inspiration is always there awaiting those who can SEE!

21. BEGINNING LIFE JOURNEY

From your first breath as a baby, you begin another journey through time and space to a destiny which is known only by your inner being.

To the infant, the world is cold and strange, and it is mostly aware of its discomfort. But the way has been prepared for another adventure and the setting comes to life.

The journey you are beginning has never been made before and the world you will find is a brand-new experience created for YOU. YOU are the center of this world and you will find that it was custom made for YOUR very special story.

You are not alone, however, for there are many others there who will provide the lessons you came to learn. There are also many from the Spiritual world to help you along your way. I too am within everything you see and everyone you encounter. This, then, is our special world.

Regardless of the paths you will choose, you cannot depart from my ways or become lost. It is YOUR response only, which evaluates your journey; you are FREE to make it what you will, but those around you are also learning and growing – all toward the same goal. Everything has meaning, but it is YOU who interprets it – there are NO accidents, for all was foreseen.

You will encounter nothing in your world which lies OUTSIDE your knowing. It is only a matter of choosing that which appeals to you; It is all valid and will lead you all ultimately in the same direction. When you finally grasp this, you will no longer fear. You have met each individual you will encounter... before. But usually in completely different circumstances. Today Life is ETERNAL and the possibilities are endless!

22. WHERE PURPOSE HAS BEEN ESTABLISHED

Life without purpose is as a journey without a map. This is however a matter of CHOICE – the one has a goal and the other is open-ended.

One way is not necessarily better than the other, but simply reflects different attitudes. Your EXPERIENCES will be in keeping with your choice, for you are always guided and assisted according to YOUR desires. Many of you CHOSE to be here at this time in order to participate in the great change which is now occurring. Many will be able to return home to their Source – their Creator.

It will be the result of an ancient desire which has guided them along the pathways of this journey through Creation and their experiences have been many and rich. But they have managed to follow the still, small voice within.

It will be a time of great rejoicing which EACH will come to know, but it has been according to choice, for all are EQUAL in the eyes of the ONE. Each is dearly loved, for each is an ASPECT of God. Each is following a pathway which was created by IT to experience ITS OWN Creations. One pathway is not right and the other wrong, but each is completely UNIQUE.

The ways of the ONE exist in complete DIVERSITY, for the ONE is INFINITE. There are no limits or restrictions – only complete FREEDOM. The Truth of this understanding is a challenge to the mind of man, though it does provide an insight as to His progress on this journey. Understand that all is in perfect order, and that God is ALL THAT IS. YOU are ITS Only Begotten Son and you are ONE WITH IT. ALL IS ONE.

23. THE TRUE DOORWAY IS ONE

If you have made your will one with that of the Creator, you need never question the possibility of its fulfillment for IT IS A CERTAINTY.

You will, in truth, be sacrificing nothing, for ITS will is YOURS.

It is within this bond that the greatest joy and happiness are to be found – regardless of outer circumstances. It is in the RESISTENCE to this idea that disharmony and imbalance appear and as you well know, dis-ease also finds its source in this condition.

It is never a question of punishment, but simply a matter of being in a state of disharmony which will eventually lead to a search for THE WAY. When one lives in HARMONY with his life's purpose, life becomes rich and rewarding.

Hatred and fear never find their way to his doorsteps, for there is no entry for them into this dwelling place. The DRAMA of the outside world is seen and recognized for what it is and no longer has any appeal to the soul which has its eyes focused upon a far greater treasure.

You may search every corner of the earth – every hermit's cave, every temple, shrine or church, but you will find no truth which will lead you more quickly to your enlightenment. Enter now into God's Great Peace and Love. Only ONE is the true doorway.

24. YOUR AWARENESS IS YOUR STAGE

Your own AWARENESS then, becomes the stage upon which the action of your personal drama is played out.

This is the world YOU create and into which no other ever gains COMPLETE access. To you it is real, as are the others who participate in your story. You see them in a light in which they CANNOT see themselves.

They are living the life YOU allow and assign to them. YOU reign supreme in this world of yours. It occupies no SPACE and has ONLY the limits and borders YOU set.

As your ideas change, however, so does your world. But it is YOU alone who brings the changes about. Some of you eventually become aware of the true nature of your world and begin to form it more in keeping with your IDEALS.

As a result, the scenes begin to change as do the players, though they STILL have only the reality YOU grant them. The actual difference is only one of PERCEPTION. The more you become aware of the true nature of your mortal existence, the more you begin to approach the question of your origin and destiny.

Where, then, is your true home and how did you get here? Where are you going when you leave, for YOUR world will no longer exist apart from the records you leave in that great hall? Your life, then, is exactly what YOU choose to make it. There IS no one else to change it other than YOU. Real growth begins when you open your eyes to the true nature of your being and begin to assume the authorship of your life. The doorway to eternity is ajar, and you now see that you are, and always were FREE...though you never realized it.

25. GENEROSITY

Do you realize that in your own life and world, those around you have ONLY the reality that YOU grant them?

It is sobering, but true. How generous ARE you? Have you ever wondered how near your generosity approaches that of your Creator? This is just another example of how YOU create your OWN lives and world. Naturally, your daily experiences will be in keeping with that which you ACCEPT to be reality, but your only TRUE limits are those you place upon YOURSELVES as well as upon others. It follows as the day does the night, that this will form your picture of the world and of life, itself.

Can you imagine to what extent it might change as you manage to alter your OWN perception? Not only will YOUR world grow, but also that of those around you. You always experience in one way or another, the results of that which you create. How flexible ARE you? Is your world large, or is it small and narrow? It is only YOUR decision. In the eyes of your Creator, you are completely FREE to create that which you desire, for It has given you the choice. You cannot look to others or point them out, for in truth, you are not seeing THEIR weaknesses, but only your OWN.

FREEDOM is a difficult concept for those who are NOT free, for they are immediately drawn into the problem of how to control others for their own satisfaction. This occupies much time and requires considerable energy, and yet, it is a completely futile approach. You have not been granted the ability to do this, thus your frustration becomes ever deeper. As you finally begin to grasp the understanding that ALL IS ONE, you will free yourselves from this torment. It is up to you to become a wise creator. You will recognize your success through your own experiences.

26. IT IS ONLY ONE

Like definitely DOES attract like. It is a Spiritual law and has naught to do with duality, for it leads unerringly to ONE.

Perfection in its ULTIMATE sense, does not exist. For this would imply the end of Creation. And ALL THAT IS, IS THE CREATIVE FORCE ITSELF IN ACTION.

The complete extension of this CONCEPT is unfathomable by the human mind, for IT is eternally in a state of becoming. Creativity is life, and EVERYTHING is alive. The intricacy of your "physical" world is but an IDEA in the mind of God.

The world of ILLUSION concerns the ROLES you come to play out on this stage. These roles are NOT your real life, but only offer opportunities to experience your creations. This is by no means apart from God but is actually the CREATOR ITSELF experiencing ITS' Creations through YOU. The element of UNCERTAINTY provides the catalyst. ALL THAT IS, is ONE. There is no "evil" involved in this process – but only CREATIVITY.

That which you perceive as "evil" is also in the state of BECOMING. As we have said, the vastness is incomprehensible to man. It is through the acknowledgement that EVERYTHING is indeed contained within ALL THAT IS, that IT assumes ITS actual place within Spiritual REALITY. It is futile to oppose this truth. Though the world does APPEAR to be filled with "evil", it has no reality as such. When your eyes become ONE, so will your world.

You are completely free to accept any aspect you choose to experience, but it is only when you begin to understand that your experience is YOUR choice, that your life will become one of Peace and Love. This understanding is your enlightenment. You do not in truth, RETURN to God!

27. A RECAPITULATION

The unmanifest is, then, master of that which IS manifest, for IT is the Source of everything.

The Matrices for every possibility were formed as the First Act of Creation and are eternal and ongoing.

Physical manifestations occur when each is called forth. It is a joint venture, for man does, indeed, have an active part in Creation.

Nothing EXISTS which does NOT have its origin in the Mind of THE ONE.

APPARENT chaos occurs when mankind misinterprets and uses these creations for selfish purposes, but careless creation must also be experienced, and man continues to learn and to grow.

Nothing is lost or damned, for the Creator is endlessly patient and all is in order. The wisdom and power of THE ONE are INFINITE and not in any way subject to the whims of man.

That which the Creator created is in the ultimate sense PERFECTION, itself.

Distortions are to be found in that which man calls time – but time exists ONLY within the mind of man.

28. THE CENTER OF THE UNIVERSE

Each one is truly the center of his universe, for he finds himself poised between its outer "limits" and the innermost reaches of his own soul.

The one appears as remote to him as the other, and yet they are the same, for they are indeed ONE. They are both the SOURCE and the GOAL.

The vastness is the vastness of the CREATOR, ITSELF, for not one reaches beyond ITS limits.

Perhaps the only impossibility would be to lose one's self OUTSIDE ITS bounds, for they are the "limits" of REALITY.

When seen from a single perspective, man appears to be completely isolated – in exile, and yet, he is in the center of everything that exists. He is as near to any achievement or goal as any other, for everything is equal in the mind of GOD.

Not one is further from his CREATOR than the other.

As we have repeated, ALL IS ONE. GOD IS ALL THAT IS. You do, indeed abide in complete peace and love. You must only accept it.

29. THE GOOD OLD DAYS

Deep within, you long for the more spiritual days of your past – for that time when you were closest to your Creator and to other souls who were dear to you.

You do not see or realize that you are now – at this moment at the spiritual PEAK of your existence and this is true for each of you.

The "good old times" you so deeply long for are the moments you are actually experiencing NOW. Never has there been more or deeper Spiritual activity than you are now experiencing.

Your eyes are still not beholding the Truths you are experiencing each day, and your nights are filled with encounters and activities of the DEEPEST Spiritual significance. You are still unaware, for you have no true point of reference. Never have your lives had more Spiritual meaning and impact on others than at this time. The children everywhere are answering the call and are beginning to seek God AND each other.

The depth of your sleep has left many of you drowsy, but you HAVE responded, and the words ARE being heard. They are written upon your hearts and you will ALL recognize them when you hear them.

They are quite distinct from the other words you have been hearing and ALL will come to know they are from the CHRIST MIND. This was the message the Christ came to declare, though it was quickly changed and hidden from you. You have been told to rejoice that you are living at this time, for you are now on the eve of the most Holy event your world has seen. Open your hearts to those around you, THEY ARE YOUR

BROTHERS. Very soon you will Know YOU ARE ALL ONE. ONE IS ALL THAT IS. Come in great Peace and Love.

30. THE POWER OF A SIMPLE BLESSING

Man has gone to incredible lengths and extremes in search of power with which he can control others.

Your history has been stained by the blood of those who have struggled with these issues, for you ALL come to eventually experience the results of your actions. It sorrows me deeply each time I see it begin once more, for its consequences will extend far beyond the battleground and, as always, will lead you far from your intention.

Your insistence upon this solution has cost you dearly and yet, many of you still do not see the folly of your ways. You concern yourselves deeply with the blasphemy you perceive in others, but you do not see what YOU are committing in MY name.

The faults you so readily observe in others are but your OWN. It has always been so, though you do not recognize it. It is not possible for YOU to change MY image of your world. You cannot break my laws, for they are immutable – my laws are LOVE.

You can ONLY alter your perception and this I granted you. It is your only solution and will create the world you are seeking. When you raise your hand against another, you are attacking YOURSELF, for YOU ARE ALL ONE.

If you raise your hand to another in a blessing in my name, you have discovered the greatest power I have granted you. Go forth in my great Peace and Love and create the world you are SEEKING. THIS, unto thee, I grant. AMEN!

PART IV
DIVERSITY

31. ACCORDING TO HIS BELIEF

To each, it will be according to his innermost belief.

The millstone of THE ONE grinds exceedingly fine and the bread will result according to the grain. The song of the flute or the harp is also according to law and figs do not grow on cucumber vines.

Spiritual laws cannot be broken.

EACH must assume the path of its NATURE.

Seek not to make flour from grapes nor wine from wheat but let each manifest ITS truth.

The fields of THE ONE are not limited to man's beliefs but abound in PLENTITUDE.

Seek to know GOD'S will for YOU and YOUR place in Creation will be secure. See that what YOU manifest is according to God's will and not the whims of man.

Oh, ye of little faith, why do you waste away in your mad efforts to override THE ONE? You must allow each to follow his OWN truth. For him, there IS no other.

If you could accept THIS, you would indeed, be this very day in paradise.

Open your eyes and your ears. GOD IS ALL THAT IS. Go in Great Peace and Love. ALL IS ONE.

32. TRUTH IS INDIVIDUAL

We have been stressing to you the value of your own inner guidance system. It is your one true contact with the Spiritual realm.

It is well to read and to study what others have experienced and learned, but it is only within YOURSELF that YOUR answers will appear. True it is that what another says will sometimes apply to you also; however, that which comes from WITHIN is intended precisely for YOU. We have been stressing from the beginning of our work with you, the infinite DIVERSITY of ALL THAT IS and this also means that YOUR truth is not necessarily the same as another's nor is his for YOU. It is not a matter of being special, for you are ALL truly special – thus your truth is also.

You cannot be compared with another, for there is NOT another who is the same. Your unity lies in this fact – you are all EQUAL in your DIVERSITY. You are all – each and every one, a different aspect of God. You are that facet which ALL THAT IS desires to experience for ITSELF. Each one of you, IT thought worthy of ITSELF, thus also worthy of YOU.

Do not judge what another is doing – regardless of how outrageous it may APPEAR to be. You have little possibility of understanding IT completely for you do not even understand yourselves. You can only know that IT is all part of a Creation which contains IT within its ENTIRITY. This is the faith you must have if you expect to truly LIVE in this world. Regardless of ITS appearance, ITS beauty, ITS simplicity or complexity; regardless of how appealing or appalling, IT is a part of ALL THAT IS.

In order to really live, you must understand and follow the

"rules". Then and only then will peace profound cover the earth and REAL joy fill the hearts of man.

33. THE ETERNAL DANCE OF LIFE

The efforts you put into any project will always provide benefits which extend beyond your expectations.

In effect, no efforts are without their reward, for as we have been saying, they send their ripples far out into the ethers of time and space and touch others who would seem to be far removed and completely unknown to you. Everything affects everything else and all responds as ONE. The old concept of duality becomes lost in the unity of TRUTH, thus your every thought and intention are important to all.

We have been showing you the infinite scope of the interweaving, implicit in all of Creation. The "tapestry" which it creates reflects such form and organization as you could hardly imagine. The richness of its texture and beauty could perhaps be described as the composition of an ultimate celestial symphony – which in truth, it is.

Its sonorities and colors, however, are not fixed, but fade and blend continually into each other with the eternally changing rhythm. It is the highest expression of beauty and joy, of melancholy, sadness and despair, of pain and anguish, and these blend into the most intense of expressions. Every emotion, every theme is essential to its composition.

No consonance or dissonance is out of place – no stress or anguish, no hushed or placid phrases. This is the symphony of Creation – of life, itself, in its fullest, most complete work. It is a landscape which completely exceeds the artist's brush stroke or the searching for words to express the poet's deepest longing. Your own theme, whatever it may be for the moment, is always included and speaks in ever changing, ever interweaving phrases of inexpressible depth and vastness of range. This is the ultimate.

34. EACH IS UNIQUE

There are many, many factors which are combined to produce the unique tonal character of any type of musical instrument.

Moreover, each instrument created by a particular craftsman will also have its INDIVIDUAL characteristics apart from its being identical in appearance. This appears to be especially true in music, for man is often so very sensitive to these sounds.

Each instrument is the product of a craftsman whose skills enable him to design the prototype, select the necessary materials and tools, and to painstakingly apply his craftsmanship to create an instrument which will respond as precisely as possible to the skills of another artist. This is all brought about not only by the physical abilities of the craftsman and artist, but also through the great love and dedication which motivate each of them.

Without them, the most ideal materials and labor would be insufficient to create a masterpiece. The sound of each will always be unique to that particular instrument and as long as it exists, that characteristic tonal quality will remain. Every piece produced will be one of a kind but will always reflect the love and skill of its creator. Those who know these sounds recognize them immediately and cherish them greatly, for they reach so deeply into the depths of ones very being. This same analogy applies to OUR Creator who fashioned each soul. The design is perfect for each particular instrument, and the materials used were from his very BEING. Each and every one was formed to produce the exact "tone" needed to produce a perfect ensemble. Each slightest variation is necessary, and there is none which is imperfect or flawed. They all blend together to create the most glorious harmony.

35. THE FOUNDER'S ART

Each will respond only to the bell which will call him to his own belief – the others, he usually will not hear.

For HIM, they do not exist, though this does not mean they are not ALSO tolling.

As man grows and develops a "keener" ear, he becomes aware of finer, more subtle sounds and they begin to draw his attention. The LOUDEST bell does not always have a beautiful sound or a truer pitch, for many are the overtones and harmonics which alter its color and its nobility.

With time, the tolling of the old bell begins to lose its appeal as the newer becomes more FAMILIAR and man learns to appreciate what he is hearing.

And, so it is with the word of God as the blatant sounds are slowly silenced by more gentle, truer ones. The older no longer has its former appeal, for now it is found to be LACKING in something which is essential to its purity.

A new experience has now begun, but it was there all along. It is often a slow process until a real search begins for the perfect source, but then you WILL find it, for you will understand for what you are seeking.

36. ANOTHER VIEW OF HISTORY

The experiences you are approaching have already been written in the hall of records and from this perspective, it is possible to retrieve information for a better understanding of what is happening NOW.

There will however also be a certain amount of 'bleed through'. Such is the nature of Creation. Your own experience of it will change this story to an extent. Each of you in his own way changes the history of his "own" world.

In any sense of the word, your own experiences of a situation...your history, will be different from that of another. You, each one of you, lives within his own private world.

Everything everywhere is in a constant state of change. Any recorded event is, in a manner of speaking, only a snapshot which will evolve and expand. This renders it impossible for anyone to capture the full meaning.

On NO level, then, is your history really accurate. Everything is eternally in the PROCESS of becoming.

Its images and sounds will continue to echo down through Eternity, and you will never CEASE to be influenced by it. In the course of Eternity, you will experience each event from EVERY possible angle and perspective, though its complete meaning will NEVER be exhausted.

In every sense of the meaning, you will come to EXPERIENCE the results of your actions. This has, however, no connection with karma.

37. INNER MEANINGS AND MESSAGES

You must grasp the inner meanings of these messages for as we have said, they are being given to you on several different levels. However, there is an overriding picture we are attempting to create within you which will give you an understanding – though without words, of your basic REALITY.

These are indeed marvelous times and the Spiritual activity is unprecedented in your world. It does all tie together in quite unsuspected ways. Never scoff at another who sees things differently, for his way, too, is right and in order.

Each will receive what is right for his continued Spiritual growth and the overall Spiritual world then becomes more completely expressed. It has been the failure to ALLOW others to seek their OWN way which has brought so much grief into your world. If you will only look, you will see examples at every hand.

Now is the time to release the threadbare ideas of control and to move into a new, much freer world of true integration and peace. It IS being done and it IS being accomplished regardless of outward appearances. Each has a part he must play, and the roles all mesh-together to form something entirely new.

Do not fear, but go along joyfully, for you too are included. You will become more and more aware that those around you are not your enemies, but simply other aspects of YOURSELF. You will find nothing there which is beyond your OWN range of experience.

Refuse to spend another day in judgment or in criticism, for you are only condemning yourself – something which God has NEVER done.

You must always allow OTHERS to seek out that which

speaks to their level, for it will lead them in the easiest manner to their OWN unique place in Creation.

Rejoice that this is so – for it was from the beginning. Man has remained too long in the lower classes of judgment and criticism and this is becoming a major issue in your time.

In the acceptance of these truths, the old world of control fear and war will dissolve, for it has far outlived its time. The dawn of a new reality is sending forth its crystal rays of light into a world which is awakening from its long nightmare of horror and fear.

As we have said repeatedly, have no fear for all is in order.

If you could only see the inner longing and hopes of those around you, you would be left completely free of judgment. Do not hesitate for a moment to express love and concern for another, for it will speak more eloquently than any negative minister of "truth".

Step forward and take your place. It has been prepared for you from the very beginning. Completely disregard the cries and the old litanies which are fading away into the echoless vastness of time. The time has come and gone and now the "new", stands bravely on your doorstep. You may open to peace and in goodwill, and all will be as it should.

Everything is related. GOD IS ALL THAT IS. Go this way and never depart from the knowing of THE ONE.

38. THE CURRENT MIGRATIONS

The Christ Mind is far more active in your world at this time than most people have any idea.

True Spirituality is becoming a major concern for people the world over and the changes ARE becoming apparent everywhere. Man is beginning to recognize HIMSELF in others on the other side of the earth and this SHOCK of recognition is beginning to crack the artificial walls of separation.

The changes which are soon to appear will exceed by far your deepest imagination. People everywhere are weary of war and chaos and are beginning to long for true brotherhood.

Do not dismay at the migrations which are so apparent, but understand them as visual TESTIMONY of the searching, which is prevalent everywhere, for many there are who understand that their old world of narrow thinking and restrictions was not the answer. They are deeply searching just as are you. Make every effort to see them as brothers. Their words may be different, but the meanings are very similar. The ground is fertile and ready for new seeds. Try to see each immigrant as one whose desire for change was intense enough for him to take enormous risks in an attempt to find a better life.

AT THE DEEPEST LEVEL, however, THIS SEARCH IS SPIRITUAL though they may NOT realize it at this point. The changes are occurring very quickly, and you will truly see God's hand everywhere you look. Your every effort toward peace and brotherhood will be assisted and YOU will also be guided. Open yourself to the Spirit of THE CHRIST and go your way in God's Great Peace and Love. All is in order. ALL IS ONE.

39. YOUR OFFERING TO THE CREATOR

An open mind and a willing heart are perfect tools in the hands of the Creator, for they can respond with precision to its' will.

In bringing ones' self to this point, you are presenting all that is necessary. Only true faith can make this possible – THE ONE never requires more. It is only necessary to hold one's intent clearly in mind – the rest is up to God.

40. WHERE DO YOU DWELL

Each day finds you in the process of LIVING or of REWRITING your history. You are, indeed, the author of your story and you can make it a true work of art.

Eternity is to be found in the moment and the moment IS your reality. You are, in truth, BYPASSING your life when you attempt to return to the past or to project into the future.

They do not exist as you imagine them to be. Perhaps this was the significance of the comment 'let the dead bury the dead'.

Where do YOU dwell? Do you even know? The question is by no means so pointless as it might seem, for it will present you with a better understanding of the true meaning of life.

Life is to be lived and experienced WHERE IT EXISTS. Do you live among the living? Do you know the DIFFERENCE?

For many of you, life is not at all what you TAKE it to be. The Master came that you may have life and have it more abundantly. What could He have meant?

PART V
JUDGEMENT AND JUSTICE

TOPICS

41. JUDGEMENT AND JUSTICE

ALL THAT IS, is the ultimate REALITY. It makes little difference what man thinks... for ITS REALITY is implicit in every aspect of Creation.

Your response to this Truth is indicative of how far you have come and how far you have yet to go. When you can look upon ANY individual or situation with full acceptance of this fact, you are approaching enlightenment. You must remember that your approval is not necessary to the functioning of God's Will. Another's truth is not required to be the same as yours.

The ultimate meaning is that you are EACH intended to have a unique and yet completely valid experience of Creation. It is the process whereby ALL THAT IS experiences ITS own Creations. You can never begin to understand the whys and wherefores.

God's sense of justice is far different from man's insistence upon immediate retribution, yet it is in perfect response to the situation. There is never any punishment involved, but only an experience of growth. You become completely free when you can accept this without judgment and condemnation, for then you can relax in the knowing that all is in Divine Order.

All is functioning as it must, and you are exactly where you should be in keeping with your understanding. It is not necessary to seek or demand justice in the way you approach it. It comes automatically to those who understand it. When you finally release yourselves from the bondage of JUDGMENT, you will then become free in a way you could never imagine. The world itself will become paradise in your eyes.

42. TRUE JUSTICE

Without an understanding that life is ETERNAL, you can have no understanding of justice.

Your ideas of justice are always centered upon ONE lifetime, thus they CANNOT achieve their goal. The purpose of life is to experience, to learn and to grow, and as you do, you always retain that which you have gained, for it becomes a PART of you and helps to guide you into the next phase. True justice can only be seen with this understanding, but it is too precise and thorough to be achieved in ONE lifetime.

You are neither judged nor punished for your errors, but then, what is to be learned without lessons? They are always necessary, and it is pointless to attempt to avoid them.

It is, however, your own choice to seek the UNDERSTANDING of what you have created, for the results are far more extensive than are thought. SPIRITUAL laws are eternal and cannot be broken and will always bring you into a greater understanding of love. I never judge, for there is nothing to judge. My justice is unfailing. Erroneous concepts of justice can never achieve what you are attempting to do and will fall away with the changes which are occurring. Only TRUTH can make you free and the True Commandments are written within you. You will never gain from another's loss, but only through love and understanding.

The day of judgment is the day when YOU evaluate for YOURSELF that which you have created. Its lesson will be clear, indeed, for you will feel its results within every atom of your being. This understanding will abide with you forever. Seek not to impose YOUR sense of justice upon another, for it must always come from within EACH of you. You have made judgment a bitter lesson and you are still suffering greatly from it.

43. ARE WE ALIKE

You may ask "if we all have the same 'spark' of God within us, aren't we alike?"

This would seem to be the case, except that in REALITY, it could not be so. We are each an INDIVIDUAL spark. Our Creator does not exist in uniformity, but in DIVERSITY.

We truly are God's body, for IT experiences ITS creation through us. Through ITS Creative DESIRES, ALL THAT IS came into Creation. Everything – every POSSIBILITY was foreseen and came into existence in the realm of possibilities and choices. Nothing exists besides this. We are, therefore, truly a part of GOD.

To take a closer look, everything that exists beside our-selves IS GOD. We are then, in a manner of speaking, God's "Only Begotten Child" – and yet, so is EVERY other living person...but God remains ONE. This is the true answer to our problems.

It is an awesome responsibility, for it changes the meaning of our lives if we can recognize it. The true vastness of ALL THAT IS, is beyond our comprehension. When we consider the implications, we can, perhaps, realize the pointlessness of trying to compare ourselves with others.

Each is UNIQUE. There is not, nor has there ever been another exactly like you.

Each is an irreplaceable part of the whole. We do not see this, however, nor do we see the futility in attempting to destroy or kill another. ALL IS Eternal. We have always been and will always be. We have free will in the choices we make, but the possibilities have already been created. Projection plays no true part.

Nothing we could ever say or do could be a surprise to ALL THAT IS. In truth, all is in order, it is functioning as ALL THAT IS created it – nor could it do otherwise.

44. PROJECTIONS

Any enemy you may encounter is ALWAYS a projection on your part. Just as with a shadow, you need never look far for its source, for it always reflects your own state of consciousness.

Enemies always come in varied shapes and sizes and usually perfectly match a given situation. Instability and fear are often the motivating forces which inspire these projections.

The problem, whatever it may be, would be most easily resolved by examining your OWN situation. Such projections become very real and menacing, often consuming the thoughts and energy of those involved.

When ones' "house" is not in order, there will ALWAYS be an enemy available to assume the cause of the difficulty.

How much grief and anguish could be avoided by taking a closer look at ones' own problems. Regardless of how logical and obvious a situation may appear to be, enemies ALWAYS appear by invitation.

Granted, they may also have their own reasons for accepting the invitation, but it is YOU who is the host. It would be wise, indeed, to take a much closer look from this point of view. It could quickly change your world and your lives.

Go rather, in Great Peace and Love. The choice is actually yours.

45. THE ALTERNATIVE

As you are now beginning to realize, the simplest way to release yourselves from the cares of the outside world is in the acceptance of the fact that they exist and that they are included in the UNDERSTANDING that GOD IS ALL THAT IS.

You neither have to approve of nor accept the cares as your OWN, but only to acknowledge their existence.

The acceptance of your OWN reality as a part of ALL THAT IS, then, does not put you in opposition to this Truth, but places you, instead, in a more POSITIVE relationship.

If it is done in complete faith, your perception will become quite different, for you will then behold a completely different order of REALITY.

It is HOPELESS to rage against and to resist what you do not understand, for your perceived enemies will appear to be invincible. When you finally come to understand that there, in truth, IS no enemy, you will experience a complete change in your consciousness.

More and more of you are now beginning to feel that your world is in a hopeless situation and yet, the solution lies within YOUR reach. The choice you will make will be based entirely upon how deeply you truly desire to know and to serve your Creator. This is the understanding of the commandment "Thou shalt have no OTHER gods before me".

This means that God is ALL THAT IS and that all is ONE.

46. IT WILL HAVE THE REALITY

Do you now see where we are going? In effect, YOU are the author of your story. And it is YOUR creation.

If you truly desire a "better" life, then YOU must live it. You must never attempt to assign YOUR responsibilities to another, an organization or your government. To be responsible is to be true to YOURSELF. By doing so, you are contributing the best you have to offer to the development of your world.

Your honesty finds its source in your being honest with YOURSELF. And your "SOURCE" is always within you – ALWAYS WITHIN!

If you do not like what you see in the outer world then you must go WITHIN to change it. Bemoaning the condition of the world around you will never bring the world you DESIRE, nor can it ever be yours...at the expense of others.

There is only one SOURCE – ALL IS ONE.

Whatever you create or do, you are doing to YOURSELF. Perhaps, then, there IS some merit in being "selfish".

It is up to you. Go in God's Great Peace and Love.

47. YOUR JOURNEYS THROUGH LIFE

Your journeys each night often take you to other realms of existence of which you have no earthly recollection, yet most often they seem quite natural to you and you question them not.

You are a frequent visitor and the sights ARE quite well known to you. In your waking state, it can be difficult for you to believe that you do indeed have connections there or that they could possibly influence your daily lives.

Your involvement as a soul reaches far beyond your imagination, for you ARE connected to others who remain completely unknown to you here. Your lives are ongoing and Eternal in the most-vast sense of the word.

You are, in truth, ALWAYS alive, though perhaps not on earth; however, as a spirit, you visit here also.

On a deeper level, these contacts DO contribute to the richness of your being for you are always meeting aspects of yourself. There are always correspondences or connecting points, and your true "background" is far, far more complex than the simple understanding your day to day life permits. Yet each one of you IS different, for your experiences are never exactly-the-same. Your lives are deeply colored in ways you do not understand, and this contributes to your uniqueness as a soul. Your brotherhood is based upon something far deeper than the paths you have traveled, and it can never become lost in your experiences.

You are ALL extensions of God. Each one experiencing different aspects of ITS creation and retaining these experiences as your own individual journey. But you are, in truth, only ONE. ONE IS ALL THAT IS. Go forth in God's great Peace and Love.

48. TO EXPERIENCE MY DREAM

It is my greatest joy to see you awakening from your illusions of the world. Your sleep has been long, and these illusions have hidden the REALITY of your being.

You have always been FREE, but you have allowed your freedom to be hidden by the outside world. When creation is limited in any way, it is no longer TRUE creation...and my creation is BOUNDLESS.

The paths creation takes are beyond number, but they are all a reflection of my desire to experience my dreams through YOU. WE ARE ALL ONE – there IS no other. Your time is mine and it is endless. You can only perceive the whole by concentrating on ONE. It can never be seen in its parts.

I knew you well, long before the beginning.

Your every step was mine and your eyes have beheld that which we formed together. I have been with you every step of the way. Your music is the sound of my Creation itself. There is nothing you can do which falls outside my knowing and it is all eternally in the process of becoming something new. It is all a part of our journey together. Your experience will be that upon which you concentrate, and this is always YOUR choice and has always been. You are always FREE to release it and to move on to something else. You will experience NOTHING we have not created together – every idea and every possibility. It is all there, but this journey will lead you into LOVE which is the GREATEST experience of all. You have been blessed and you abound in my grace. It is up to you to CHOOSE, and your CHOICE will determine your experiences. Each is different, but one is not better than another, for they all lead to the same goal. You are

FREE, you are dearly loved, and I am with you always. WE ARE ONE.

PART VI
FREEDOM

TOPICS

49. WALK THE PATHS OF PEACE

Walk always along the paths of peace. Never mistake it as a lack of conviction or courage, for it WILL demand much of you.

It can only become REAL to you when you slowly begin to view all as ONE.

Intellectual comprehension can open the way, but you must actually begin to FEEL and to SEE unity. By no means do you withdraw your support for peace, but you expand it to include ALL your brothers.

As we have repeated, your decisions are all arbitrary and have naught to do with God's Will. You MUST come to grasp the sanctity of ALL of life in order to even begin to comprehend the true nature of peace. Every living thing deserves your recognition and respect as a Creature of God. Any approach which would suggest otherwise does not reflect the will of the Creator.

You are NEVER justified in relegating your OWN responsibility to others, for if they were responsible, they would never demand it. To learn of God's truths, you must always turn WITHIN.

They will be your ONLY source of peace. Everything else is but illusion and will simply continue to lead you down the well-worn path of history as you know it.

How much does peace MEAN to you? Is it worth a closer examination of your beliefs? These are your only possibilities. Which do you choose?

May you walk in God's Great Peace and Love. ALL IS ONE.

50. THOSE YOU ENCOUNTER

Do you ever wonder about the different people who have crossed your path in the course of a lifetime?

Did any of them have any real meaning, or were they simply chance encounters? And what about the circumstances that brought you together? What were they, or do you know?

Many have appeared and were as quickly gone as ships in the night, though you never forgot them. Others were there for long periods of time – perhaps years, yet you were hardly aware of them. Then it suddenly occurred to you they had gone – yet when, you did not know, for they barely left an impression. Acquaintances bud and blossom into friendships, but often they bear no fruit. Do these encounters have any meaning – any true meaning, or are they simply chance happenings?

There are also those you feel you have known always – have you? In a sense, there are fewer mysteries in life which are more perplexing. And yet in some way, you feel there IS a meaning. As we have repeated to you – THERE ARE NO ACCIDENTS. There is nothing which was not foreseen. There IS ultimately meaning or significance in EVERYTHING though perhaps, most often, you are not sure what it is.

The influences which direct your lives are INFINITE and most of them are subtle, indeed. Your greatest gifts often come in very small packages, but you cannot determine the true value by its size or initial impact, for this can be very misleading. Our constant refrain to you has been to keep your eyes and ears open and to remain in the moment. You miss many things and events which are highly significant to you. Countless opportunities present themselves but pass you by completely unnoticed.

51. CREATING, INTER-WEAVING, CHANGING

And you pass your days in wonderment and in questioning, for there is much which you behold, but do not understand.

The possibilities of interpretation appear to be endless, and yet your mind seems to demand a specific answer – THE answer. But this answer never comes, for before you are able to grasp it and file it neatly away in your memory, it has begun to lose its clarity and definition and to take on another appearance. And so-it-is with the world around you – though even more so with your own EXISTENCE. It sometimes feels hopeless, to fully comprehend the meaning. This appears to be the lot of man, for he alone can ASSIGN the true meaning of his being, but this meaning also blurs and begins to take on another appearance with each new day, encounter and experience.

That which in truth is COMPLETE FREEDOM becomes overpowering and often frightening, for you have become accustomed to a certain rigidity in your mindset.

You believe that you LONG for complete freedom, though you cannot accept the TRUTH that it is ALREADY yours. How could you look to another to choose its ultimate meaning?

This IS its purpose. I do not judge, I create, I experience and observe, for my curiosity always demands another and yet another view of my Creation. The endless possibilities which I behold lead me ever deeper into my desire to create and to experience the results. The most minute aspect is exciting to me, for it is an essential component. For me also, there is no final definition, since the slightest variation changes the whole into another view. To me, it is all beautiful beyond description, it is awe inspiring and Sacred and this is ALL THAT IS. Open yourself to it and enter in!

52. THE TRUE ANTICHRIST

LOVE can only begin to make an appearance in your world when you overcome JUDGMENT, for it is, in effect, the ANTICHRIST... you FEAR.

It is judgment which brings about and promotes separation and duality. You must come to love YOURSELF before you can accept and begin to love another.

GOD IS LOVE and speaks to Its children through the CHRIST, thus none can come to the Father save THROUGH the CHRIST. For HE IS GOD'S MANIFESTATION IN THE PHYSICAL WORLD.

Sin is SEPARATION. Though it does not really exist but is only ILLUSION. You are NEVER alone but are always surrounded by many who know and love you. They ABIDE in the Spiritual world and are alive in the Eternal Now. Behold. I have told you a mystery. Let him who has ears . . .

53. THE CHRIST AND THE DEVIL

You still search everywhere to find another who is responsible for your OWN choices. But YOU have in every sense created the life you are experiencing.

You have been granted complete freedom as well as the greatest gift of the gods, for you are creators with UNLIMITED possibilities.

The world is a creator's SCHOOL, for it is here where you learn how YOUR choices affect OTHERS, as well as yourself and all of Creation. You are completely free to choose anything you desire, but it ALWAYS becomes YOUR lesson, for you will experience its result in every sense, but it IS a lesson and never a punishment.

That which you allow for yourself, you must also allow for your brother. You are ALL equal in the eyes of God; there ARE none with special privileges – neither prince nor pauper. ALL ARE EQUAL.

Religion has made a scapegoat of the CHRIST, but He did NOT come to absolve man from his responsibilities.

It is never ANOTHER entity or race that is responsible for YOUR lessons. There ARE no victims. Peace will come to those who learn that the world is indeed a school, and that ALL are required to learn their lessons.

54. THE PRISONER

Man does not see that the chains which bind him to the walls of his cell are of his OWN making.

They are the ever-expanding negative thoughts which grow – each from the other, connecting him ever more securely to a past which, in truth, NO LONGER EXISTS.

He does not see that they are not real and that he has fashioned them himself from FEAR – the hardest of substances. To him, they are real, indeed, as is fear, itself.

Nor can he unlock them until he can see that their reality is only what HE gives it. With the passing of each day, another and yet another link of the chain is completed, slowly restricting him to complete immobility.

How can we convince you that you are FREE?

There ARE no chains strong enough to bind God's Only Son who prevails even over death, itself. Why can you not see that your FATHER has granted you COMPLETE freedom?

The same power which enabled you to CREATE your chains can also allow you to CHANGE them into acts of Love and Gratitude. Look once again. In the depths of your heart do you really see iron, or do you see FEAR?

Only YOU can know. It is only YOU who gives it its reality. Take up your pad and go in God's Great Peace and Love.

55. CONTROLLING AND USING THOUGHTS

The issues with which you concern yourselves are not always the truly important ones.

If you were to employ the energy you expend each day on your Spiritual development, you would become spiritual giants. Your priorities will eventually form your lives and the results will most probably NOT be those you are intending.

It is YOU who chooses your thoughts, but this must be done carefully. If you simply allow them to appear at random, this then will be your EXPERIENCE.

True, it does require mental discipline to learn to select and control your thoughts, but it is a necessary step in creating the experiences you would hope to have. It is as if by magic that wherever you place your attention, that is where you will find growth – either positive or negative.

It is very easy to gaze out upon your world and see what the future each is creating will hold for him – though this has nothing to do with paranormal abilities. You are being handed the keys to the kingdom and it is up to you to accept them and to apply the correct one to unlock your treasures. NOTHING APPEARS UNBIDDEN.

Many of you are now beginning to awaken and to assume responsibility for yourselves. Regardless of appearances, what you were taught is not how your world functions. The true message of your Creator is that you were, indeed, granted freedom of choice, but YOU ARE RESPONSIBLE FOR YOUR CHOICE. You cannot make ANOTHER responsible for you. Therein lies true freedom, and as you have been hearing, YOU

ARE FREE. Your Creator is wise enough to realize that some of your efforts will have severe consequences, but this is necessary in order for you to become a TRUE creator. Everything which ALL THAT IS creates, also creates.

You are truly blessed by each one and NOT cursed or damned to eternal punishment. You are growing. Your experiences come ever more into harmony with a beautiful life as the result of your choices. It is a very effective teaching process and one which should interest you deeply at this time. Consciously accept your challenge – you will rejoice when you do.

56. YOUR SEARCH FOR TRUTH

If you are sincere, your search for truth will always lead you along the paths of the less familiar – it will always initiate change.

To seek and to change are inseparable. You must first of all come to see that life does NOT function as you have been led to believe and you must be willing to examine EVERYTHING which presents itself in a completely objective light. Nothing can be excluded.

Many of your older concepts are erroneous, and thus, your understanding is distorted. The REAL power of Truth is never diminished thereby but will come into its own. One area of attention will suggest another and if you are diligent, you will eventually become free in a way you could never before have conceived.

Real growth and creativity can only be realized in complete freedom. These limitations were not imposed upon you by your Creator, but by those seeking power. In order to regain your freedom, you must become RESPONSIBLE for yourself.

You ALWAYS lose when you assign your freedom to others.

As children of THE ONE and as co-creators, you were intended to live in complete FREEDOM. This is ruled by Spiritual law, not by man. Man's laws have now placed most of the world in chains and the chaos you are now facing is the inevitable result. The Christ comes to tell you that God's laws are engraved upon your heart and that ALL will come to know them. Your quest for truth will always lead you WITHIN. When you seek, your life will change. Go forth in God's Great Peace and Love. ALL IS ONE.

57. UNDERSTANDING YOUR TRUTH

It is inevitable that when one is truly seeking his path, he will become confused by much seemingly contradictory information.

As we have explained, each of you will have his OWN truth which will not always be in accord with that of others. In a sense, there is no ultimate point of view, for your paths and experiences are each UNIQUE. Your truth will always be confirmed by the resonance it finds within you.

As you progress along the way, your views will always change – they are, nevertheless, your truth. When you always attempt to make your will one with God, you need never fear.

You are intended to enjoy life and to rejoice for each new day. For each is indeed, a gift to you. You can become lost very quickly if you attempt to find your way simply by following rules and laws. Accept the best each day has to offer and be willing to LEARN from your mistakes. They occur for a purpose.

You must remember however that this applies to your brother as well. Leave far behind any negative approaches which can serve neither you nor any others but will only bring suffering and misery. That which is TRUE will be for the good of ALL and never at the expense of others, for this will ultimately not be positive for you either. Your own rights will also expand as you grant the same to others around you. They can only diminish as you attempt to exempt yourself. You will always know deep within if you are in harmony with your purpose, for it will be reflected in your life as well as in your body. Your optimum growth is achieved by bringing your entire being into harmony with your understanding of your Creator. You cannot do more. Always go in God's great peace and love. GOD IS ALL THAT IS.

58. MAN'S CHAOS IS GOD'S DIVINE ORDER

Regardless of the outward manifestation, each one you encounter is another aspect of ALL THAT IS – thus, another look, at YOURSELF.

When you awaken to your own Truth, you will begin to recognize yourself in everyone you meet.

Each one is a necessary encounter in coming to know YOURSELF. Each presents an opportunity to expand your consciousness and to embrace life in its totality, its complexity and ultimately...in its simplicity.

The shock of recognition can indeed be overwhelming, but EACH one is included within THE ONE. Your efforts to ignore this or to separate yourself from it are self- defeating, for you will remain fast in a world of duality – a world of right and wrong – good and "evil".

Death and destruction are its rewards. When you eventually accept life on its own terms, you step into the ETERNAL NOW.

Everything does have its place and its purpose and man's apparent chaos is then recognized as God's Divine Order. It is but a question of perception, but it is a step each must eventually take.

The days ARE growing short. Open your eyes and your ears and seek the voice WITHIN. Your way will be guided, and you may go forth in God's Great Peace and Love.

59. QUESTIONS

Your INNER world and experience IS the valid one. It is the distilled ESSENCE of who you really are, and it is Eternal.

As everything else, it too, is ever changing and becoming.

This morning, you are not the same person who climbed into bed at the close of the past day, nor are you the one who left home to begin a life of your own. In THIS sense, neither did you reincarnate into this life, for you are a DIFFERENT person, with a different outlook and a different name. But then, who are you?

If this is true, (and it is), how can you ever hope to FIND yourself? This presents a far different picture than the one you have grown to accept. Are you "YOU" when you are "good" or perhaps when you are "bad", or neither?

But then, THESE concepts also change constantly. At what point, then, are you really "YOU"?

The same applies to those who ATTEMPT to judge you. From what point are they making their judgments? How then, could they be valid? Nor once again, can YOU judge yourself? Or another? It becomes ever more obvious that life is an experience – but whose? Can this be established in time or space, for it is apparently something more?

For this same reason, you could hardly accept what ANOTHER assigns you. If all of creation is continually in the process of change and becoming – then what could it possibly be? It is a valid question and one which concerns you, too. Do you consider it to be worth asking? Can you accept the answer?

60. THE NEED TO QUESTION

How can one expect an answer if he does not question and yet, this is how so many live.

A small child usually realizes this, and his questions abound though they all too soon begin to diminish. Is this because he has learned all he needs to know or because he has not really been answered?

Is there no REAL curiosity about life?

If one learns only what he hears, he will never grow beyond the LIMITS of those around him. Every individual is UNIQUE in Creation and abides in his own Reality.

He must seek his OWN pathway through Creation, for the ways of the outer world CANNOT answer his innermost needs. It is all too easy to resign ones-self to the ways of the world, though there will always remain an unfulfilled inner longing as the growth of the soul eventually stagnates.

If you only knew there is one WITHIN who is ALWAYS there and able and willing to reveal the words that it longs to hear.

THEY ARE HIS TRUTH.

61. RULES

To bind yourself to the letter of the law can never bring you to righteousness.

The rules actually appear AFTER the fact...which is the reverse of man's understanding.

Yet we must remind you that each has his OWN truth.

Then concern yourselves rather with the idea of seeing YOURSELF in each one you encounter – regardless of who he is, and the rules and laws will begin to fall by the wayside.

What is to be DONE is a far more positive approach than that which is to be avoided. You ARE in truth, FREE, but your brother is also. By limiting the freedom of another, you are (once again) limiting YOURSELF.

Maximum growth is to be achieved in coming to understand that ALL IS TRULY ONE. It is a far more direct path than concerning yourself with rules.

On that day when you can look out on ALL of Creation with complete understanding that GOD IS ALL THAT IS, you will be completely free and rules will no longer have any meaning.

> The letter killeth,
> But the spirit giveth life.
> Christianity

62. AN OVERVIEW OF LIFE

We can each only come to know God as IT reveals ITSELF to us and this is a never- ending process. God is INFINITE and each of ITS Creations is unique.

All of ITS Children are ONE in that we are equal ASPECTS of Divine energy. We were, EACH of us, created as a completely unique Aspect of a Creation which IT has chosen to experience through us.

Our missions in life are Spiritual and we are each primarily Spiritual beings. Every experience in our lives is for the purpose of learning and growth. It is completely pointless and hopeless to attempt to define and outline what is acceptable and what is not. It will be governed automatically by God's Purpose and in ITS time. We can best grow and benefit from this by basing our lives on our INNER guidance. It becomes more obvious each day that any system of rules and regulations is hopeless because there exist only exceptions at every level, and THIS is the Law, itself. We are not only free, but we are "condemned" to freedom. It cannot be otherwise, for there could be no Creativity.

We are, each one of us, in exactly the place where we are intended to be at this time. There is no safety possible other than in the Divine Order. We must each find it for ourselves by opening ourselves to the REALITY of who we and our fellow beings ARE. The world appears dark and the WAY indistinct because we have fashioned dark glasses to protect us from the LIGHT. In the bright light of day, shadows are clearly visible, and the way becomes clear for all to see. We can remain in the dark for as long as we wish, but there are those who are opening their eyes to another world which was there all along. They are beginning to see the world clearly for the first time.

63. THE LAST FRONTIER

It may not be a new idea, but the last and greatest frontier does, in fact, lie WITHIN. THERE will be found the gateway to your future and to your true FREEDOM.

The limitations and restrictions of the outer world begin to fade away when man realizes that he has the power to either accept or reject them. True growth and creativity can only exist and flourish in COMPLETE freedom and in this inner world you BECOME the law which guides your life. There is no truth which will NOT withstand the Pure White Light of examination, but it will actually emerge with GREATER strength.

There is nothing so holy as to be exempt, for you are INTENDED to grow in your understanding. Once you journey beyond the borders of the outside world, you will open yourself to the REALITY of your inner guidance and you will begin to recognize the words that are intended for you alone. The doubts and fears which have always diverted your attention and energy will no longer have the reality you have previously accepted, for you will now behold them in another light.

The only remaining limitations will be those of your own imagination which will begin to grow and expand in its new-found FREEDOM. How quickly you will come to see that in truth, you were ALWAYS free, but that YOU had accepted the limitations and rules which have placed you in bondage. Your closest contact with the Creative Source is WITHIN.

You will NOT be entering "dangerous" or "forbidden" territory as you have been led to believe but will begin to tread the paths of the illuminated ones who have contributed so much to mankind. Your first true step into the INNER world will become one giant step for man. May you go forth in God's Great Peace and Love.

PART VII
REVERANCE FOR LIFE

64. THE SANCTITY OF LIFE

What is worship but the recognition and acknowledgement of LIFE – ALL OF LIFE, for it is sacred, indeed. ALL OF LIFE IS THE MANIFESTATION OF ONE.

You are never apart from your Source, for IT is ALL THAT IS.

Your attempt to divide and qualify IT are blasphemy, and it is your failure to recognize this which has brought so much grief into your world. Spiritually and physically you are One with your brother as you are with me.

It is your RESISTANCE to your knowing which is the source of disharmony in your lives and in your world. There is nothing you can say or do which can change this truth, for it is immutable.

Your worship means nothing unless it is in Spirit and in Truth – all else is dogma.

I require no sacrifices or adoration and your flattery is offensive. Your LOVE and your happiness are my greatest joy and your experiences and growth are mine, also. I demand nothing more.

This understanding will bring the birth of the Christ. It is approaching quickly. Prepare yourselves.

65. THEIR WAYS ARE IN ORDER

I know those who seek to do my will and our bond becomes ever stronger. I am aware of every thought and word which is given for OTHERS.

You will be guided in your every effort and your days will be filled with the sense of my presence that you may know that I am with you. ALL are mine and ALL are enfolded in my love.

I reject NONE.

Do not despair, for all is as it must be. Man is NOT, nor was he ever lost.

Your experiences are, indeed, your own choice and your INNER being well knows who it is. It is not your task to re-form others. They are experiencing exactly that which they NEED to know, and their ways ARE in order.

Know that WHATEVER you behold, I had already conceived. You, too, are exactly where you will grow MOST.

Your love must become strong enough to encompass ALL and you will be UNTOUCHED by that which does not pertain to YOU. As you have so often been told, you have absolutely nothing to fear. You must feel FREE to seek me in those around you, for I am most definitely there. Do not recoil at the "evil" of the world, for all is perfect.

Pursue your life in Great Peace and Love, for they are yours. ALL IS ONE.

66. MAKE EVERY ENCOUNTER SACRED

Intentionally make each contact you have with another a SACRED event, for regardless of the apparent level of its nature, it is, in truth, just that.

This is not to imply that it should be of an emotional, sentimental nature, but that it must be sincere and to the best interest of each.

Little do most of you realize the complexity of the chain of influences you set into motion with each encounter and activity, for it extends far beyond the actual contact, itself.

The most significant effects may not appear for some time to come, though they WILL manifest whether you are consciously aware of them or not. When you initiate a relationship, you must expect it to REGRESS to you in its effect.

The outside world is never the CAUSE, but only a mirror reflecting the hidden meanings or significance of YOUR actions. The observation and understanding of this Truth will go far, indeed, in improving your relations with others.

This is a spiritual law and is immutable.

Ultimately, there are no gains to be made at the expense of another, regardless of your perception, for what you sow will always return to you in its kind. It is never karma as you understand it, but only a most effective learning situation. When you strive to consciously make each contact a sacred event, it will become just that. You will continue your way in God's Great Peace and Love. ALL IS ONE.

67. EACH

Each one who enters your door does so for a reason – though it may not always be completely conscious.

You must realize that each in his own way is searching for the meaning of life and inwardly feels that they may possibly hold a key. Each is an opportunity which moves in TWO directions – it does not stop with YOU. You do not see the incredible range of possibilities which a single knock on the door can initiate.

EVERYTHING occurs for a purpose – NOTHING is random.

Remain CONSCIOUS in each MOMENT, for each is offering you an experience as well as growth and LOVE.

You cannot always visualize where it is leading you or what the result might be. To remain asleep results in "rest" and inactivity. FULL consciousness UNITES each with ALL THAT IS. And ETERNAL LIFE – IT IS ONE!

68. THE WORD AND THE LIGHT

All of creation declares the wonders of God, for it was fashioned by ITS boundless love and creativity.

ITS magnitude within your world has by no means been grasped or understood. ITS precision is staggering indeed, and the most insignificant aspect is OVERWHELMING in its meaning and importance. And yet, IT forms a whole. IT IS ONE.

There exists nothing which is not included within ITS unity. Divisions in reality do not exist. They are imposed by man in his attempts to understand, but it is a futile approach. Nothing can be grasped apart from ITS COMPLETE state.

There, IT will be seen in its TRUE holiness, for EVERYTHING is a reflection of ITS Source.

Why do you wonder that evil APPEARS to lurk behind every corner? Do you not realize that sin means separation which does NOT exist, other than within the mind of man? This is the true message of the Christ – the Anointed One.

The deaf do not hear and the blind do not see, but The WORD and the LIGHT are becoming increasingly more intense. When YOU become whole, you will become ONE, then you will know that GOD IS ALL THAT IS. Go His way in Great Peace and Love.

69. THE PERFECTION OF ONE

You are never apart from the beautiful and what is truly inspiring. Wherever you may find yourself, you are always completely surrounded by the most beautiful and profound.

You have only to open your eyes a little wider and to observe and listen more intently. There is no aspect of Creation which when seen in its WHOLENESS is not incredibly beautiful.

It is only your insistence upon fragmentation and duality which is distorting your perception. When anything remains ugly or repulsive to you, you may be sure you are not seeing it in its fullness of being.

God's Creations are faultless, and EVERYTHING has its place.

If you were able to see creation in its entirety, its vastness would be completely overwhelming. How your lives would change if you were to begin to approach your world with this understanding. There is nothing to be found which is unworthy.

Your ideas of good and bad, right and wrong are arbitrary. Real LOVE and profound peace can only abide with the acceptance of the world AS IT IS. Your problems would all melt just as the snow melts in the warmth of the sun. Do not moan and cry out to God to correct your world, for there is absolutely NOTHING to correct. Your real understanding of this TRUTH is actually your lesson – your purpose in being here. Strive, instead, to make your WILL that of the ONE. This is where your pathway is leading, but it is YOU who chooses your journey. They are all, in truth, ONE.

70. CYCLES OF NATURE

In your world of rapidly increasing change and devolution, the cycles of nature continue, and each year enfolds as ordained by your Creator.

Trees are now beginning to change their colors. The shadows lengthen and each day becomes shorter as the sun takes on a golden hue. Crops have matured and the harvest has been gathered into barns. The fields will now remain empty as the year begins to close on another cycle of life – and yet, growth has not ended, for the preparation has already begun for another round.

Each autumn, as each other season, bears its own stamp and differs from the one which preceded it. As the leaves which fall from the branches, no two are identical though they carry the same name. Each is the result of countless factors which have come together to create an experience which was UNIQUE and a harvest which was the fruit of many combined laws and effects. These cycles are repeated endlessly to continue the development of each species.

Growth is the purpose of each, and each continues to CONTRIBUTE to the expansion of creativity. As man interacts with the laws of creation, he experiences DIRECTLY the results of his part.

Each attempt brings to his doorstep the harvest of his efforts. He is still learning how his actions affect his world and yet he must continue, for he has not reached "perfection" after numberless attempts. The cycles of Spiritual life are not otherwise, for each one presents a harvest from the seeds which were sown, but the efforts continue, and creation is endlessly patient. Each gain benefits mankind and opens new possibilities for ALL. Nothing is truly lost, for there is ever a new beginning with renewed hope and promise. This is the LIGHT.

71. THE REVELATION OF SCIENCE

Although these words were penned so many centuries ago, they contain the wisdom which still guides man today. ALL THAT IS, is not beyond knowing and will reveal IT-self to those who are truly seeking.

The TRUTHS which were granted to man from the beginning still echo loudly down the halls of time. They are proclaimed today as the latest revelations of science, but this has always been so. The CREATOR, the universe and your world are far, far different from what you have been taught, and the TRUTH is infinitely more vast, and all-inclusive than you have any idea.

When you are finally released from the bonds of ignorance, you can never truly return to the limitations of the past, for your journey is ever onward. Continue to open your windows ever wider to the LIGHT of universal wisdom, for it will move you swiftly into the realms of Peace, Love and Knowledge.

The curse of bondage and ignorance will fade away in the Light of truth. There is no religion – only TRUTH and LOVE, and their Light is beginning to dawn brightly in your world.

It will serve you greatly that science is confirming many of the truths of the ancients, for it is from THIS point that you will accept confirmation of what has been denied you. Open yourselves to the greatest revelation of all which will be proclaimed to you by the still, small voice WITHIN. Its words will literally thunder the message intended for YOU. Fortunate are you when they begin to fall on your ears for you are then beginning to dwell under the shadow of the Almighty. You must not only hear these words, but you must also MAKE THEM YOURS – For they ARE yours, indeed. Move quickly into that place which has been prepared for you.

72. THE SNOW

The Great Peace and Love of THE ONE falls slowly and silently upon the sleeping world as does the snow on a long and dark winter's night. But man continues to slumber and is completely unaware of the changes in the outside world.

He receives no physical sensations to announce these changes but will open his eyes the next morning to a sparkling new world. The dreariness of winter has vanished, and a different reality has appeared.

And so it is with the coming of THE CHRIST into your world.

Man has been asleep, and the world is indeed changing virtually overnight. He will awaken to a world which presents quite another picture.

Although he well knew that it was a possibility, the appearance of the snow was nevertheless a surprise. You HAVE been told of the changes which are approaching, but you too may well be surprised at how silently they are occurring.

But man continues to slumber...completely unaware of the changes in the outside world.

73. TO POINT THE WAY

Kinship with all of life is the mark of the mystic, for well he knows that all is ONE.

He does not feel called upon to prove it, but only to point the way for those who are moving in this direction. There IS no possible proof for those who know ANOTHER reality, for this has no existence for them.

It is not amiss to allow each to answer his call. In so doing, he remains precisely where he should be, and everything is in perfect order. Answer our OWN calling, then, for it is the one INTENDED FOR YOU.

By remaining in the Eternal Now, you will always be on course and your journey WILL be your own truth. Relax in the knowing and acceptance of these words, for they bring great peace and understanding.

The God of your heart knows you well and always provides the means for your way.

The true mystic does not seek a literal truth, for he knows he is working with probabilities and change. He is carried along by the stream of consciousness which flows from the Creator.

The choices are YOUR responsibility and have naught to do with the outside world. Make YOUR will one with GOD'S and you will always go in Great Peace and Love.

PART VIII
LIVING IN THE MOMENT

TOPICS

74. SPONTANEITY

As human beings, you continuously receive bits of information both on the conscious as well as on the extended levels of your consciousness.

Much of this information alerts you to upcoming changes which may affect you in one way or another. It covers an enormous range of possibilities and enables you to live and to function in the moment.

As you learn to respond to this subtle communication, your lives become ever more spontaneous. The precision of the timing of these contacts, possibilities and events provided for you by the unseen world is remarkable indeed and must be allowed complete freedom in operation.

These are far more than simply coincidences and synchronicities and they are calling for your closest attention.

Most often, there is little opportunity for lengthy examination and consideration, for the precision involved demands IMMEDIATE response.

Countless opportunities are lost to you each day because you were NOT in the moment. Such is the nature of your lives at this time.

Live in the moment and keep your eyes and ears open, for you are most definitely being guided. Go in God's Great Peace and Love.

75. A CONSCIOUS JOURNEY THROUGH TIME

We are striving to bring you to the point where your life will always be a CONSCIOUS journey through time and space.

Your thoughts must become involved in living in the now; your eyes and ears as well as your mind must be open and receptive, and you must take conscious control of your life as well as your responsibilities.

THE VOICE OF THE CHRIST SPEAKS TO ALL WHO WILL HEAR and it will guide each-and-every one of you on your way. There are NEVER any true conflicts in His message, but only in your understanding.

When conflicts SEEM to appear, seek within for the answer.

Allow your life to take the direction of your OWN choice rather than that of the outside world.

You came with your OWN purpose. Why, then, allow others to direct your course – they cannot know what it is. What we are saying will require a definite decision and commitment on your part. Make it your gift to yourself as well as to the world.

The sleep which has fallen on mankind is now being disturbed by restless nightmares which are causing much fear and uncertainty.

TRUTH is now pouring into your world from many who are receiving our words. Your future will be what you choose it to be. You are not only free, but you are REQUIRED to make a choice in one manner or the other. There is no other possibility. There is no one else who can do this for you. There is a future for you.

What will it be?

76. LIVING ON MORE THAN ONE LEVEL

When you have learned to function consciously on more than one level, you have reached the point where true Spiritual development can begin.

This same ability allows man to begin to FUNCTION on OTHER planes as well.

The actual REALITY of your being far exceeds that which is familiar to you and the more Spiritual aspects can begin to be understood in a new light.

This ability will offer man new hope in a world that appears to be in a hopeless situation. Your possibilities exceed by far those which your present understanding allows. These abilities are now beginning to appear in your world and the upcoming changes will move mankind into another realm.

Begin to open yourself to the meaning of these changes for you will be deeply affected by them. Go now in Peace.

77. NEW OPPORTUNITIES AND CHANGE

In order to invite new opportunities and change into your lives, you must be determined to open yourselves to...and REMAIN open to all possibilities.

One must wonder how many wonderful things have passed you by simply because you did not recognize them – in other words, you must be awake and remain awake.

As with so many things, you limit the possibilities by refusing to look for the whole. You usually see only fragments thus your lives remain fragmented.

Can you REALLY believe this is a world of unlimited possibilities or are these merely words of an idealistic dreamer? It is up to you to decide.

If you can imagine or think of something, you can achieve it.

Often, ideas occur without precedence. They must ALSO be considered. They well may be truly inspired. It is exciting to explore the realm of the unknown.

You need only keep it in mind that you usually find what you SEEK. If your goals are positive and for the ultimate good of ALL, you need feel no limits or have any fear. Your limits have been removed and the world of Creation is yours.

78. REPEATED RANDOM EXPERIENCES

Whenever you have repeated random encounters with another or with a situation, there is ALWAYS an underlying purpose.

You will usually become consciously aware of these events, for they will often strike you as being somewhat unusual.

Almost invariably, they will have something in particular to relate to you. They will often come about under very unusual circumstances.

Begin to watch for them, though most often you will soon notice their strange persistence. They can occur in so many different ways that it would be difficult to outline them.

They will inevitably bring about change in one way or another – and this is their purpose.

The Spiritual world always finds ways to contact you, but by living and remaining in the moment, you will become ever more aware of these messages. You will also become more proficient in accepting or declining them.

The most important step is in becoming aware of what is happening. Sometimes the clues can be subtle, but they can also become humorously obvious. We suggest you begin to watch for them and to analyze them, for they are certain to present a new possibility or direction.

These occurrences are endless, and it makes no difference how isolated you may be, for they are to be found everywhere. They bring movement into your life.

79. REFLECTIONS

You who are weary and are seeking rest and renewal for your souls, I will refresh you with water from the ETERNAL spring.

Many of your lands are parching and your wells are running dry while others cannot keep back the waters which are rushing out of control taking everything in their path.

Your mountains are trembling, and fear and uncertainty abound, but the outer world is only a REFLECTION of the inner. It is, then, the INNER world which is calling for your attention.

Each problem must be resolved at a HIGHER level than its origin. Seek not the answer where it is NOT to be found but go to the SOURCE.

Go WITHIN yourself.

80. THE POINT OF DEPARTURE

Establish yourself firmly in the moment. It is the point of departure.

The instant you allow yourself to STRAY from the moment, you regress to a realm which in truth does NOT exist. You are no longer living your REAL life but have returned to the world of ILLUSION.

It is indeed a shadow world, for the shadows sway and move as do those of a tree stirred by a gust of wind. The MOMENT – the Eternal moment is your ONLY contact with ETERNITY to be found within the physical world.

It is that which separates the living from the so – called dead.

Our constant admonition to you to live in the moment is far more significant than simply attempting to get your attention. You have read that the point of power is in the moment and you have struggled to grasp the full understanding.

It is far MORE significant than you might think. Do not be misled by the apparent simplicity of God's ways, for they are profound, indeed.

The "NOW" is the precision point for fine-tuning your entire being to the Spiritual world while in the physical realm. Do not pass over these words lightly or take them as a figure of speech but realize that they lead you to Eternal Life.

81. TIME

We have been showing you that time does not exist in the way you have come to believe it does.

Both the future and the past are open to you and are responsive, even now, to your influence and interpretation.

This single fact extends your creative abilities far beyond your present understanding. The most important and "earth-shaking" of all, however, is that it ALL exists within THIS very MOMENT.

The greatest truth is that THIS ACTUAL MOMENT IS ALL THAT IS.

You are constantly examining the "past" and projecting into the "future", but they EXIST only "now". There is nothing apart from this. The complete mastery of life, then, is concerned with the mastering of each moment. Everything that exists, that has ever existed or ever shall exist is contained ONLY in the smallest conceivable fraction of time as you understand it – but it is eternal.

The true secret of creation lies in coming to terms with REALITY – but what is it? Does this tell you anything about God – or creation? Life and death? Good or evil? Perhaps it explains something about the forgiveness of "sins" – but whose sins?

Where do YOU fit in? Who, then is your friend or your enemy? The questions are without number – they are Infinite. Can you see an answer? There is only ONE.

82. ANOTHER VIEW OF TIME

Each of your experiences, then, is the result of the focusing of your attention upon that to which it is directed.

In the ultimate sense, time actually does not play such an important part as you might imagine, for you CAN concentrate your attention upon the future or the past as easily as upon the present.

It is, for example, possible to concentrate your consciousness on the past to such an extent that you are indeed drawn into its reality as it exists for YOU. If this is done properly, this experience then becomes as valid as that of any other who was deeply involved. This is not nearly so difficult as it might appear, if it is done frequently, and as a result, it can remain for you a truly CONSCIOUS occurrence. This depends mostly upon your acceptance of the fact that it CAN be done and a true conviction that YOU ALSO, can do it.

Your lives are colored to a remarkable extent by these experiences, though you seldom take them for what they really are. They do become, then, an actual part of your "history" and they do actually alter your life to one degree or another.

This applies, naturally, to future events or situations as well, and as you can see, it is related to your ability to create your own future. As we have said, both the past and the future are malleable. You are by no means limited to the one-way flow of the clock and calendar as you now believe, but you actually have access to the INFINITE to a far greater extent than you can now conceive. The ONLY validity of any event or experience is that which YOU take from it. It is by no means ever chiseled into stone as you have been led to believe.

More Views On Time: THE PROCESS OF "BECOMING".

The most insignificant happening actually changes the whole to some extent.

This may appear to be meaningless in the scheme of things, but the combined force field becomes ever more potent as it continues to grow and to form that which is being suggested.

You, personally, constantly receive bits of information on an unconscious level. This combines to expand the energy in a creative chain and to accelerate the actual formation of each creation in physical reality.

It can become a highly significant tool in your hands when you consciously begin to experiment with these concepts, for they are by no means deluded dreams of those who are deranged, but highly effective techniques to expand your consciousness and your physical, as well as your Spiritual lives. We suggest you begin to make them yours. With your first single success, your world will change forever, and you will never again accept the old bonds of limitation.

83. PRACTICE LIVING OUT OF TIME

The concept of time is but another limitation YOU have placed upon your lives. It restricts you in many ways you do not as yet understand.

You are, in truth, much nearer to ANY event in history than you imagine and many of your associations with the "past" continue to this day. By experimenting with your concept of time, you can extend your sense of freedom in ways that will be very beneficial to you – and especially in your creativity. Rather than dividing your life into periods of time, you might think of it as points of FOCUS, thus one "period" becomes as near as any other, regardless of the time frame ASSIGNED to it. Your relationships will also take on other significances. This practice would be very beneficial at this point and you would also be able to accomplish more. You are indeed ETERNAL and are by no means actually limited by the ticking of a clock. Make every effort to remove self-imposed restrictions and begin to assume your TRUE, identity. You are a child of the UNIVERSE.

WHERE DO YOU DWELL?

Each day finds you in the process of LIVING or of REWRITING your history.

You are indeed, the author of your story and you can make it a true work of art. You are, in truth, BYPASSING your life when you attempt to return to the past or to project into the future, for they do not exist as you imagine them to be. Perhaps this was the significance of the comment 'let the dead bury the dead'. Where do YOU dwell? Or do you know? The question is by no means so pointless as it might seem, for it will present you with a better understanding of the true meaning of life. Life is to be lived and experienced WHERE IT EXISTS. Do you live among the living?

84. MASTER THE MOMENT

Your relationship with others will come to change and take on new meanings as you come to know and to ACCEPT who you are.

The new understanding will be seen through the eyes of THE ONE and with the TRUE equality this will reveal which will be unlike any intellectual understanding you may have had in the "past".

It will be experienced in a twinkle of an eye – a moment.

It will not be necessary to project it into the future, for the future completely dissolves within the INFINITY of this moment. This INSTANT is all you are required to completely master.

It will suffice to establish God's Kingdom on earth and the reign of true peace. It is in THIS moment that all hatred and fear can and must be released and this single act will release YOU from the eternal hell of your OWN creation.

It is in THIS moment that the ONE all are seeking will appear. All will recognize and know, for this will be ALL you behold. It will occur in the twinkle of an eye – in but a MOMENT.

85. SPACE

Space, like time, is by no means as rigid or set as you conceive it to be.

In a sense, you might think of it more as a projection screen upon which the images of your daily life are projected.

These IMAGES are yours only – no one else sees them in the same way as you. This is your private world. Within this same "space", however the images of the REST of the world also appear. The "distances" which separate you are quite different than you might think.

YOUR world is "created" AROUND you when you begin your earthly life and remains until you leave it again. Just as with radio and television signals they occupy no actual space as you think of it but coexist within the same realm.

The projection techniques are remarkable, indeed, and give the impression of "reality", but in the truest sense, they are illusion. They DO provide a perfect stage for the drama and for the role you came to play. As we have said, you are the center of this universe and the action revolves around YOU. You are truly the star and the others form your supporting cast. However, the same is true for each of the OTHERS.

From this analogy it is a simple step, indeed, to parallel worlds and universes – all played out in what you still may refer to as the same space. The end of your world comes as easily and as naturally as it began – as a jump from one channel to another. Your TRUE reality is APART from the play, though you become so absorbed in its contents and action that you no longer remember. But who is the observer of these performances? Since he does not appear to be present, where is he? What is the purpose? How do the dramas then relate? These are the basic questions...

86. A CONTINUOUS JOURNEY

It is up to you to become aware that you are indeed alive in EACH moment, though they are, in truth, seamless. You are already THERE, but you must awaken to its REALITY.

The death you so fear does NOT exist.

You leave your world behind at the close of each day and awaken within a completely different reality. After a relatively short period, you return to your previous state of daily existence. There is nothing mysterious about it to you.

You always retain traces as well as memories of the past night which continue to color your lives. You are in any given moment the result of the total sum of your experiences.

You deceive yourselves when you attempt to DENY these experiences on ANY level, for they do indeed, BELONG to you. They are REAL and they are important to your growth and understanding.

Little do you grasp the vastness of the CREATOR experiencing ITSELF through YOU.

You have been blessed far beyond your understanding. Go forth in ITS Great Peace and Love. IT IS ALL ONE.

87. CONCENTRATE ON THE ETERNAL

It is a good practice to seek and to concern yourselves with that which is eternal.

You may think that this would be very limiting, but it is not. When you begin such an activity, you will find more and more which will present itself to you. Much that is trivial and unworthy will begin to fall away from your life and you will begin to feel more secure and confident.

Many things which you have HELD to be permanent have been disappearing from your world, and you have found that they were ILLUSION.

Man needs stability, but THE NATURE OF THIS REALM IS CHANGE. Perhaps precisely for this reason you must realize that CHANGE, itself, IS ETERNAL.

Eternity is contained within each INSTANT, as fleeting as this appears to be.

Those things which you discover to be ETERNAL, will always bring you CLOSER to ALL THAT IS.

This practice will awaken in you a deep feeling for that which is truly important, and you will soon begin to see things in a different light. Make every effort to stretch your consciousness in every direction. Your life will grow in direct relationship to your awakening. You will see much that you never realized existed, and your life will become immeasurably richer.

Do not mistake the fear of tasting Life for Righteousness. Life, as with the flame of a candle, can only bring forth its Light by fulfilling its purpose . Where there is no activity, neither is there Illumination to Lighten the way for you or others.

88. ON MUSIC

When you listen to the music that appeals to you so much, you are being affected by much more than frequencies, or pitches, but also by the emotions and memories they create within you.

These feelings, however, extend far beyond your own range and also include those of the composer and his life, as well as his past lives and racial memories. Memories and emotions originating from the Spiritual realm are also included.

The combined impact of these vibrations can indeed be overwhelming, for they reach so deeply into the soul and excite responses to memories, sensations and emotions long forgotten.

How often it is that you cannot account for the intense, yet highly intimate reaction it evokes within you?

Music is indeed, the universal language, but you often cannot grasp the strange connections it awakens. Needless-to-say, the more subtle the composition, the more it often contains.

The real gift of the composer lies in the richness of his own inner experiences and in his ability to incorporate them into the vibrational frequencies with which he creates.

The true Spiritual nature of music is not limited to so-called Spiritual themes, but includes the vitality of life, itself. The depth or quality of the music of a people is a direct reflection of its Spiritual development. Exposure to great music is a wonderful way to bring growth into your own life, for it WILL become ever richer as a result.

PART IX
TURNING WITHIN

TOPICS

Where Words Fail
The Word
Everything Speaks
The Secret Path
The Journey

89. MAKING YOUR DAY

When you awaken from your night's sleep, you can either accept the mood which remains from your dream world or select another in keeping with the attitudes you wish to establish in your life. The choice is ALWAYS yours.

This is another example of how easy it is to allow your life to form by default. If you observe your thoughts, you will quickly begin to see how limited you have permitted them to become. You must realize that it is YOU who selects them.

Most of you would not consider wearing the same clothes each-and-every day and yet your thoughts have still more influence. As we have said, ANYTHING you create always begins as a thought or an idea. The range of your life and your activities is a reflection, of your states of mind. It is, in truth, no more difficult to look through your usual "list" of subjects and select a mood or attitude you would LIKE to experience each day than it is to select the clothing you would find to be ideal for a particular occasion.

Whether you choose by default or by selection, your experiences will most definitely be colored by YOUR choice.

If you truly desire to become the captain of your voyage, this is an ideal area in which to begin to assume your role. You seldom realize to what an extent you turn the direction of your lives over to others around you. If you keep your eyes and ears open and intentionally LIVE each moment, you will be amazed at the growth you will experience. It would be a sad ending to your role to finally realize that it was actually not YOU who lived your story, but others you allowed to make your choices. This is not the will of your creator, nor in the DEEPEST sense, is it yours. YOU ARE FREE.

90. PEACEFUL BEGINNING FOR EACH DAY

It is ideal to begin each day in great peace and expectation. Happiness comes far more easily to those who are quiet and peaceful.

These are both traits which you, yourself, must develop and they will accompany you on each step of life's journey. They are two of life's treasures and will continue to reward you as time moves on.

Peace comes with the knowing that God is with you always and that all is in order. It is YOU who chooses your responses to life. Both of these traits are highly contagious and can be passed on to others around you. You may rest in the knowledge that they can be easily acquired and put into practice. They will quickly change your outlook from one of hopelessness and fear to that of real happiness and enthusiasm.

This will cost you only some deep concentration and the willingness to change your perception. When you begin such an endeavor, you will also be assisted from our side.

Always remember who you are, that you too, are a creator, and that you have complete freedom to CHANGE your life. Any trait which has come to you from the outside was ACCEPTED by you at one time or another, and it follows that it can also be CHANGED by you.

You are not the helpless VICTIM of the whims of others, but you are in charge of your own direction and course. This will be put into action by your honest decision to do so. You, as well as others around you, have everything to gain and only fear and anxiety to lose. Begin to take charge of your own life and do not depend upon the outside world to provide what is already yours. You are one with ALL THAT IS.

91. A LIFE OF SERENITY

A life of serenity becomes yours by claiming it.

In your world today, it seldom comes automatically and each who desires it must come to understand what it truly is.

The turmoil of the outside world is the result of illusion and deception, and it comes to reign when the ego gains complete control. Serenity can only abide when one has come to understand who he REALLY is, then the incessant beat of drums and the shrill blasts of the trumpet no longer call to war any who have come to see through the falseness of the ILLUSION.

There is, then, nothing whatsoever which can override the complete serenity which remains.

FUTURE growth results from striving on a much HIGHER level. This is the growth which will benefit ALL and call all of mankind to receive its true inheritance.

May the peace of God which exceeds all understanding abide in your hearts forever.

92. RELAX INTO YOUR TRUTH

Perhaps the best way we can word it is to say that you must RELAX into your truth. Your truth already IS. You must ALLOW it to form – to come into material expression. It literally means to be true to YOURSELF.

When for whatever reason you depart from it or refuse to accept it, you are cutting yourself off from the life you CHOSE to experience and, needless to say, you begin to feel lost and disoriented.

Yet it is possible to experience an alternate plan, though it will not be your optimal experience. There is nothing to fear when you are really following your Truth. Through the ACCEPTANCE of the world as it IS, you FREE yourself from many negative circumstances and can then focus your attention on that which is your own goal.

You cannot change the outside world to your liking, but you CAN find and dwell within your own – they can, and do, exist side by side. Nothing comes into your life unbidden, and nothing can touch you without your ACCEPTANCE. You are free.

YOU ARE FREE to experience that which was intended for your own growth and benefit. Your truth is as vital and important as any other and only you can bring about a change through your own thoughts and acceptance. It is most important to you that you remain focused on and dedicated to your deeper desires. They will continue to serve you – even during this period. In any given situation, there is always a solution or choice which is for your best and it will always lead you to the next step. You have been given the "gift of the gods" in your ability to create your life to your own liking. Some are fortunate enough to know this instinctively; others must bring it into their own consciousness...

93. ACHIEVING SERENITY

How easily and how swiftly peace begins to prevail in the lives of those who have released the major stumbling blocks.

Real serenity can never come to one who is torn by judgment and its twin – division. It is always a losing battle, for it is not based upon REALITY.

The only solution is the acceptance of the possibility that the Creator might have a BROADER understanding. Many of the lessons which have brought your world to this point have been bitter indeed, but the REPEATED responses from the past have resulted in only more of the same – each time more violent and destructive.

The true nature of Creation is diversity. CONFORMITY ALWAYS DEMANDS JUDGMENT AND FORCE.

There is an amazing simplicity in the seeming complexity of God's Ways and the concept of TRUE freedom has seldom been grasped other than by the Spiritually mature. The world's understanding bears little resemblance to its TRUTH.

Your concept of duality with its attending judgment has thoroughly dissected your world as well as your lives and now you MUST return to unity. GOD IS ALL THAT IS. ALL IS ONE. Go in God's Great Peace and Love.

94. PEACE, TRUE PEACE

Peace, true peace, must begin with YOU.

You must be its SOURCE within your world. It will extend itself to each who comes into contact with you – much as a single spark can ignite an entire forest.

It is NOT amiss to work on YOURSELF, for your influence is far reaching indeed.

You must remove the idea of limitations – they have no existence in REALITY.

Open yourself to ANY possibility which presents itself, for it is being OFFERED to you.

You may be used unconsciously, or it can also occur in full consciousness where you will benefit most.

When you sincerely ask to be guided, you may be certain of a response. Become and remain fully conscious in EACH individual moment and you will find yourself conscious in the Eternal Now – IN ETERNITY.

You will abide in Peace, and its companion – LOVE, will be yours also.

95. A SACRED EVENT

As in all things, you can make this day what you wish and take from it that which speaks to YOU.

Open yourself to the highest manifestation which your faith will permit and you will never be disappointed.

The highest possibilities exist at-all-times, but it is your own BELIEF which allows them to come forth into your life.

Include your brother in your expectations, for he will be there also. Is such a manifestation possible in your sight? Do you TRULY believe it could be?

When you enter your chamber this morning, you will present as your gift and your sacrifice that which you are leaving BEHIND as you seek to move ahead. Make this offering a worthy one – one which will bespeak your deepest intention.

It is YOU who will decide where your path will lead you this day, but this is also true for EACH day.

You can draw upon the combined energy EACH will contribute to strengthen you, but you must allow it to remain WITH you. Your Creator is not limited by YOUR beliefs but will use them to assist your own efforts.

Go this day and evermore in the Great Peace and Love of THE ONE. AMEN

96. SEEKING YOUR DEEPEST LEVEL

It is within the very depths of your being where the waters are truly still and without turbulence of any kind. It is here where you can reach the Infinite and come into closest contact with your Source, and it is here where you must seek me also.

The distractions and distortions of the outer world are many and make our contacts most difficult. It does require much effort and patience to be able to attain this level, but it is necessary for what we are doing.

Theories and explanations of the Spiritual world are fascinating but let us remind you that they are unnecessary to its actual FUNCTIONING and this is what concerns us. The amassing of endless theories avails you nothing if you are unable to achieve what you are seeking. THIS is the area where you must concentrate your efforts.

You must be able to discern Truth when it is presented to you.

This ability grows through actual contact with the unseen world as well as by remaining in the moment at any level you find yourself.

Life is truly Eternal and when you remain focused within the MOMENT, you are always in the very midst of life. This point will carry you ever onward through Eternity on a virtually unbroken path. Experiences and lifetimes blend into one Eternal experience which THE ONE has shared with you. How vastly different your view and attitude toward life becomes. There can remain no fear, for all is truly seen as ONE. INFINITY becomes your home and the terrors and disappointments of isolated incarnations give way to the supreme creativity of ALL THAT IS. This is your destiny.

97. PARTICIPATE

You are being called to PARTICIPATE in your deepest, innermost concept of your God, for THIS is the nature of the Spiritual path.

It is meaningless without your personal EXPERIENCE, for then it will have no REALITY.

Dedicate yourself COMPLETELY to THE ONE – no doubts, no fears, no reservations and you will BECOME the results of your efforts.

Knowledge is never so important as EXPERIENCE, for the one is ABOUT life, but the other is life, ITSELF.

Allow all obstacles to fall by the wayside and enter with your heart, your soul and your BEING into THE ONE. Allow IT to REVEAL ITSELF to you for IT will – IT is ever so near.

Continually ask for guidance and you will not be disappointed.

98. SEND ME

You have been called. Make your response: 'Here I am O Lord, send me.'

Make your whole life your RESPONSE to honoring ITS name.

It will speak far more clearly than words. Open yourself to God COMPLETELY and go forth in ITS Eternal Grace and Love.

The true leap of faith is that from conscious REASONING to Spiritual KNOWING.

The abyss between appears to be bottomless, but this leap is required of each at some point on his journey. It is, in effect, the approaching change of consciousness.

You WILL know when your name has been called; the change is that near.

Your pathway through Eternity is YOUR choice; you are never a VICTIM of circumstances, but the God of YOUR universe. Make your reign the HONOR you give to THE ONE. It is ALL THAT IS.

99. ON SPIRITUAL COMMITMENT

When you commit yourselves completely to the Spiritual, you will always be guided. You may trust that you will always be presented with that which is best for you and at the appropriate time.

You need never have any fear of *finding yourself,* apart from this guidance, but you must remain in the MOMENT and completely open. What you see in the world around you is not your drama unless you CHOOSE for it to be. Always fill your lives and minds with that which is positive and creative – that which you deeply desire to see manifested in your lives, for SO it will be. You have been granted a wonderful opportunity to be here at this time. Amid all the apparent chaos and confusion, a new world is beginning to form from out of the mists and will shortly appear in the freshness of spring.

Your protection lies in your CHOICES – in that which you CONSISTENTLY picture in your mind. Nothing appears unbidden or even by surprise. You may discern that which is on your horizon by carefully observing your thoughts and wishes to see if they are in complete HARMONY.

It will no longer serve to point to ANOTHER as the source of your 'problems', for your problems do not originate apart from YOU. If you expect freedom of choice, YOU, yourself, are responsible for that choice. Wake up. Wake up and see the Truth which you so desperately seek. It is all around you! It will in no way benefit you if you have another, do your 'homework'. Each one of you has so very much to contribute to your world. Never minimize what you OR another is doing, for you cannot see it in its extension. Life is for LIVING and not for possessing.

100. YOUR TRUE COMMITMENT

You must make your inner desires a true COMMITMENT on every level.

Allow your desires to become your Truth and begin at once to LIVE in accord with this reality.

It must speak of who you really are at your DEEPEST level, and your acceptance of its REALITY must be complete.

At this point, what you have asked will have already come into existence on the Spiritual level and its manifestation in your life will occur in direct relation to your degree of ACCEPTANCE.

Know that on every level, it is complete and is presenting your reality. Know also, that it will respond precisely to the actual INTENT of your desire and not to the WORDS you are repeating.

Your innermost thoughts and desires are always known and when they are in complete accord with your WORDS, they become powerful, indeed. On the deepest level, you can only deceive YOURSELF. Accept what has been prepared for you, for it bears your name and it IS yours. Use it wisely and it WILL become a blessing not only for you, but for all of mankind. You already possess the key to grant your access to the secrets of fulfilling your journey. You need not seek further but only to place it into the lock which will open for you. You must be CERTAIN that its fulfillment will be something you truly desire for IT WILL BE SO. Go in God's Great Peace and Love.

101. OUT OF THE DEPTHS

Out of the DEPTHS shall His words come to you.

This is where the Source of Spiritual activity and growth is to be found, for it is the fount of Spiritual wisdom. You are always presented with exactly that which is needed for your growth at a given time.

When a "problem" arises, we suggest you search immediately for the PURPOSE of the situation.

You will not go away empty, for everything that occurs has meaning AND purpose. It is NEVER punishment, but a blessing in disguise.

All of life is, in effect, a learning experience – regardless of what you have been led to believe. Always live with this idea in mind and your passage will become much lighter.

It will NOT benefit you to attempt to remove the problem, to cover it up or to run away from it, but TRUE growth is to be found in understanding and resolving it.

Neither do your experiences pass unnoticed, but often benefit OTHERS as well. You must remember, it is YOU who calls these situations TO yourself through your own choices and actions. Accept them for their true purpose and your outlook will respond immediately.

Go always in God's Great Peace and Love.

102. THE STILL SMALL VOICE

Fortunate are you when you begin to respond to the still, small voice within, for this is the beginning of your awakening.

You often approach me as though I were delicate or weak, though I am not. My voice, though it is not loud, will make itself known to you.

My ways are neither mysterious nor secret, for they are written on EVERYTHING you behold. They have been hidden from your eyes by those who would lead your way, though this is not what I intended for you.

Each shall know that my name and my words are also written on your hearts. I speak directly to you through the CHRIST MIND and my message is intended only for YOU. It is never contradictory but is a distinct part of my creation. You will always know in your heart if it is true, and it will lead you directly along the path you have chosen. As you look out upon your world today, it is easy to see only chaos and confusion, but you are not seeing my TRUTH. My love abounds.

My words are being heard everywhere. The diversity you behold is still unfamiliar to you – it is, nevertheless, but ONE. Open yourself to it and rejoice in it, for you, too, are included. Each of you has a very definite place within my Creation, for each of you expresses an aspect of me which I long to experience. It is all but a part of the whole and none are excluded. You are being guided each moment and all will be well. My words are intended for you and they are sufficient. Seek to understand that which you are hearing. The words will often be surprising and perhaps strange to you, but they will lead you along your path. If something seems unreal to you, it has, then, no meaning for you. Know that NONE are excluded.

103. ABIDE IN THE SHADOW

The state of oneness is actually your NATURAL state and with patience and effort, it can be reestablished in your lives.

Strive continuously to reduce the idle mind chatter which so effectively overrides the inner voice.

Your days will soon become increasingly more tranquil and more ordered. You will, indeed, come to abide in the shadow of the Almighty. Let not your heart be troubled, neither let it be afraid, for you will always be safely guided along YOUR path.

Its treasures are worthier than gold – much fine gold and your sleep will also be sweet. True peace can only come to him who INVITES it and welcomes it into his life.

Though the world be in turmoil, it will not come near you nor snare you in its trap, for it exists NOT on the path of THE ONE.

The still, small voice is always to be heard if you truly desire to hear. Rejoice that you have HEARD these words, for your path WILL be made clear and your passage a certainty.

Living waters are not to be found in the mirages of the desert, nor could they quench your deepest thirst. Drink freely from the SOURCE of all life and Go ITS Way in Great Peace and Love. ALL IS ONE.

104. REMOVING YOUR RESTRICTIONS

As you consciously begin to remove the barriers which so effectively separate you from the unseen world, you will begin to find one connection after another which draws you into new directions.

Gradually, you will begin to open and to pass through doors you never realized existed.

You will soon come to see how effectively you have been prevented from moving out into new areas of greater possibility. Completely NEW areas of interest will then begin to open as if by magic, but the possibilities will continue to expand as you allow one barrier after another to crack and to crumble away into nothing.

YOU have accepted these limits – one after another throughout your life, but you never questioned by what "authority" they were passed on to you.

All too often, they have been erected as a means of controlling society...that it not "sink into chaos". But "man's authorities", themselves, have still managed to do that very thing.

You have been granted the ability to judge what is appropriate for YOURSELF and what is not. In truth, ONLY you can know for sure.

We have repeated ever again that you ARE being guided and watched over. Your inner voice will keep you on course. Be not afraid to expand your horizon and to consciously ACCEPT your role as a co-creator of your world. You will begin to fulfill your purpose and your life will become ever richer. ALL IS ONE. Go forth in God's Great Peace and Love.

105. WHOEVER WILL MAY DRINK

Whoever will, may drink from the fountain of waters which flow freely to all. You need only to come in sincerity and in longing for that which will guide you through these upcoming days.

You will be shown that which you need to know to help you make your way easily through these changes. Put all your trust and faith in THE ONE, IT will not fail you.

The Christ spirit is once again entering your world and will make ITS way known to you. IT will speak to all who will hear and respond to ITS message.

You are living in the greatest Spiritual period your world has ever known and are privileged to take part in this event. Open your hearts and your minds – move into and remain in the moment. Keep your eyes and ears open and be a full witness to the coming of the CHRIST.

IT is near – very near and you are beginning to sense ITS arrival. Cast aside your old ideas and behold the Truth which is about to appear before your eyes. Seek IT within your brother, your enemy and within YOURSELF. You will FIND IT there. Go forth into your world with joy and confidence, for the time has come and the hour is approaching. Do not hesitate to share what you find with others, it will strengthen their faith and light their way. You need have no fear, but can go forth in full confidence, for you have already been recognized and IT will come to you.

Do not judge those who might scoff or ridicule, for their time will also come. They, too, will move forth, for they are not lost, but will move in their own time. Put aside all that may hinder you and seek only the TRUTH and the WAY. You will not go astray but will be guided with every step. Do not concern yourself with anything else.

106. ATTITUDES

It is sufficient to be WILLING to grow and to mature.

This attitude, itself will initiate the beginning of the process. Without such an approach, you are already in a disadvantaged position. Your attitude is always of primary importance in virtually everything you do, for it is almost instantaneously TRANSMITTED to those around you.

It is also quickly RETURNED in the responses it evokes.

Thorough observation and a careful study of your attitudes would go far in helping you to transform your life from one of basic negativity into its most desirable counterpart.

This will begin to place YOU in control of your life without the need of outside help.

Make yourself ...in EVERY way, a true channel for the Eternal God. ITS blessings will flow into your life in every form and manner.

Your attitude is one of your most important characteristics. Give it the care and attention it deserves, and you and everyone around you, will rejoice in the results.

Go forth then, into a new and beautiful world.

107. THE FATHER'S WILL

Our Creator always smiles upon a willing heart, and one so blessed will be called upon in some way.

That which is asked is not always impressive and demanding but is NECESSARY to fulfill a particular need at a given time. And it is THIS which gives it its importance.

His ways are not so harsh and demanding as you have been led to believe, yet His voice and steps fall softly upon the earth.

He is USUALLY not to be found in the roaring storm – rather in the quiet expectation of dawn, or in the hushed stillness of twilight.

His words, however, are easily perceived by listening ears and by those who are searching. It is most often NOT the spectacular which reveals His will; he is more likely to be found in the midst of the quiet unrest which brings His children to seek Him.

No, you do not have to go to the ends of the earth or always study at the feet of great masters to learn you Father's will, for He will reveal it to YOU through the CHRIST MIND within.

Your holiest moments are those you spend in quiet contemplation with a WILLINGNESS to do that which is asked of you. It WILL then, be presented to you. Your most elaborate words could never begin to form a more beautiful prayer to THE ONE who well knows your name. May each of your days be blessed by the great love for you.

108. ASK AND IT SHALL BE GIVEN

What you truly desire to know will be revealed to you.

You must ask in full confidence that you will be heard and answered. What ARE the questions that most consume your attention? Are they truly worthy of such consideration or are they simply curiosity?

These questions require you to take a very close look at your life. What, then, is MOST important to you? How does it affect others? How will the answer affect your own life? What lies beyond the door you wish to open?

The answer could be just the momentary satisfaction of your curiosity or the doorway to ANOTHER REALITY. Ask and it shall be given. Seek and you shall find. Knock and it will be opened unto you.

Go in God's Great Peace and Love. ALL IS ONE.

109. THE ONE YOU WOULD CHOOSE TO BE

Do you ever picture in your mind's eye the person you would CHOOSE to be?

Do you ever visualize him, study his bearing and countenance, his attitudes and characteristics? Can you imagine meeting him and getting to know him? Do you recognize him? Is he vastly different from you? In what ways?

What is it, exactly, that separates you from this person?

Are you still working toward becoming this ideal or have you given up? Don't you realize that he ALREADY exists – exactly as you perceive him in every detail? He existed even before you appeared in this body.

It is, then, not a matter of creating what has already been created but of ALLOWING him to appear in the here and the now. It is pointless to create what already exists, you have only to accept that it is already there.

You must claim and take possession of your creation. It does not mean that you cannot make improvements and slight changes, but that you must also ACCEPT yourself as you truly ARE.

The ideal model was selected by YOU for a purpose – to serve perfectly in a lifetime which you ALSO chose. When you cease to compare yourself with others and return to your own life and purpose, little by little, your chosen ideal will appear. The time will come when you will gaze into your mirror and can say to yourself "I like what I see" and you will suddenly realize that your life is perfect – it is exactly who you ARE. Your happiness and sense of peace will be profound, indeed.

110. FROM MY HIGHER SELF

That which you record this morning is given to you through your higher self as you have requested. It comes through the experiences you have accumulated throughout your existence in combination with those of your entity and your contacts with THE ALL.

This understanding then, although it is ever evolving and changing, remains your UNIQUE story.

It cannot be compared with that of another, for the details are never the same. It serves you not to attempt to accept the history of ANOTHER as your own, for it will not resonate WITHIN and will always remain foreign and unreal to you.

Your OWN story is written within the cells of your own BODY and is reflected in the outer reaches of your MIND. It is YOURS only.

The combined totality of the experiences of every living thing becomes the reflection of ALL THAT IS. IT is Eternal and IT is ever changing. This vastness can only be understood in THE ONE.

The ULTIMATE Truth lies only in this UNITY, which is still more vast than the sum of ITS parts. IT can never be grasped by attempting to dissect IT.

It is your vague awareness of this TOTALITY which fills you with wonderment and awe and it is this vague awareness which you refer to as God. It is futile to attempt to force another to accept ANY understanding which lies beyond his unique range.

Your greatest fulfillment lies in the acceptance of your OWN reality as IT has developed for YOU and to honor IT, as well as that of ALL OTHERS as truly Divine, for IT is SO.

This IS and will always remain your personal Truth – regardless of the changes and growth you will experience. The TOTALITY of Creation is, then, a reflection of the Mind of God as IT exists in each instant.

Question: What is the meaning of THE ALL? This is unclear to me.

Answer: THE ALL is used to include not only your personal soul group and your oversoul, but also its most extended range including some who are of other groups. It implies your MOST extended range of contact.

It is far-reaching although it does not refer to God as such. It is from this realm that you receive the lessons which are given in the first person. They are genuine and you can accept them.

111. SEEKING YOUR ORIGINS

You possess the ability to enter in and to touch the origins of your BEING as well as your DESTINATION.

It has never been denied you – it is only necessary to allow it to occur through your DEEPEST desire.

There IS much to be gained by observing your path and where it has taken you, for you did not suddenly appear by chance where you now FIND yourself, but by having followed a particular route through creation.

Each and every stopover has been NECESSARY on your journey. The slightest change in direction would have brought you to ANOTHER destination.

It is when you truly become aware of the results of your CHOICES that your journey begins to take on real meaning and understanding. You are always given clues, but you must watch for them. The decisions you make today will most definitely affect your direction.

It is always up to YOU to decide and to keep your eyes on the horizon. Your goal is already there, but the pathway is always subject to change.

You are FREE to make your journey exactly what you wish. The route is not, however as important as the GOAL. You should, nevertheless, choose it in FULL consciousness.

112. AN EXPERIENCE

During my morning session there was a long pause and then I went into a deep meditative state where I had the following experience:

"Yes, I do know you are there. I cannot define you, but I know I am a part of you. I am within you. I sense your being everywhere. I cannot tell where it starts or where it ends – it is ONE. I can feel myself within it – and yet I know I am separate. I am not aware of others – there seems to be no one else there. There is only awareness – no specific knowing. I cannot tell if this is the beginning (of existence), now, or in the future. It is a warm knowing.

There seems to be nothing before this – or after. I am waiting. I am expecting something to give it meaning, but there is only silence. I am not afraid, for it feels very familiar to me. It is true, it is beyond question. IT IS, and I AM THERE, TOO.

I am included within it though I do not see myself. There is no point of reference – no point of separation; it is completely boundless. It is all knowledge – all knowing, but at this point there is no manifestation – only being.

All is soft, white light. There are no sounds, only presence – there is only presence and knowing. It is from this you form your world. It is all contained here, but nothing is defined – it is only being – undefined being. There is no feeling of time or movement – only Light and Being and Knowing. This is all there is. It is you who gives it meaning.

There ARE no rules. There are no instructions. At this point there are no desires – only Being. I cannot tell what it means. There is no one to explain – it simply IS. There is nothing more to be said. IT IS ALL THAT IS.

113. THE TEMPLE OF THE ABIDING PRESENCE

My church is WITHIN. For your body is indeed, the Temple of The Abiding Presence.

They are MY words which sound forth and echo throughout your sanctuary and out into your world. I chose the most beautiful and sacred structure in all of Creation for the indwelling of my Spirit, for it was fashioned out of my deepest Love. All behold my temple and are often overcome by its beauty, but you do not realize what you are seeing and feeling, for you mistake the structure itself, as its PURPOSE, and you fail to recognize my PRESENCE within. Your efforts to create grander and more elaborate cathedrals are noble, though they completely miss the point. There is in truth, nothing in your world which is NOT sacred, for I am to be found EVERYWHERE. I have chosen, however, to abide where I could be NEAREST to you, for I love you dearly, even though you have made a recreational hall of my sanctuary and you ignore the words of LOVE and WISDOM I impart to you.

My sermons are never long and vague, but clear and precise. Your nervous songs override the deep sonority, serenity and joy of my harmony and my most sublime creation is often seen as a tavern. The infinite beauty of the world pours inside through its magnificent windows and my LIGHT guides your way. How I long for you to enter and commune with me, for I have so very much to relate to you. Oh that you would see that the Temple of The Abiding Presence is the most SACRED dwelling of THE ONE. Enter in Great Peace and Love.

Do not search in distant skies for God.
In man's own heart is He Found.
Shintoism

114. PRAYER

Prayer, true prayer is actually a state of mind. In its truest sense, it is not a request for something physical, but the sincere desire to come into complete harmony with ALL THAT IS.

It does not have to be a formal repetition of words, but it is best expressed as an ongoing attempt to find and REMAIN in the closest possible contact with the Creator. In this sense, one's life, itself, becomes a prayer.

The focus of life becomes centered on this desire and its fulfillment, and in this state, life becomes sacred as does everything one encounters – ALL becomes ONE.

It is possible to reach this state without a CONSCIOUS recognition of this Truth, but on some level, it becomes an UNSPOKEN Reality. In this sense, all prayers are answered and this desire, itself eventually begins to align one with the Creative Source.

All of life becomes an ongoing quest and it is clearly reflected in all that one thinks and does. It is not your place to judge the level of achievement of those around you, but only to recognize God within them – and this can take many DIFFERENT forms. This type of prayer never separates one from another because the quest, though differently expressed, is ONE. You must always approach those around you in this understanding and it will always lead you into the knowledge of THE ONE.

If you could but realize the value of your quiet moments, spent in prayer and meditation. Your every quest is blessed, and your world moves ever nearer to its Truth. You do not begin to understand the effects of these moments, for they are truly awe inspiring. Far more is accomplished in your chamber than in the halls. Open yourself to the guidance.

115. MEDITATION

The level of pure consciousness is that state which IS. It sees or knows no duality whatsoever. It simply IS.

It is the release from duality and the profound peace which it affords that is so beneficial to man – both Spiritually and physically.

This release from judgment and from the cares of the world is essential to finding a state of balance in your lives. As you realize, it is the absence of balance which brings about a lack of harmony and dis-ease. Meditation opens the door to the secret place of the MOST HIGH, for there, one ABIDES in the shadow of the Almighty.

There, no fear or doubt can enter in. There exists only pure being – it is in conflict with nothing – it simply observes and knows. This is, in truth, THE ONE observing Its Creation through YOUR eyes – no anger, fear or judgment – only eternal observation and understanding.

The profound peace which is to be found in meditation can also extend into your daily lives when you ALSO become observers. What you will discover will bring you into complete unity with THE ONE and your only tears will be those of great joy, for ALL will become consciously ONE and time will be no more.

GO ALWAYS
INTO THAT GREAT PLACE WITHIN
WHERE YOU FIND THE SILENT ANSWERS
THEY ARE YOUR TRUTH

116. WHERE WORDS FAIL

As often as not, words fail to convey the exact meaning which is intended, and this seems to be particularly true with the subtleties of mystical thought.

The more words that are employed, the more obscured the meaning becomes.

This is often also true with prayer and as we have said, in its truest sense, one's life BECOMES the prayer. It can be difficult, indeed, to communicate deeper truths and ideas to others or to grasp them when they are given.

Let us say, however, that the highest truths are revealed WITHOUT words. They are most often the ones intended for YOU alone and they become a definite part of your relationship with your Creator.

Each of you is unique and each one is on a very special journey which has never been traveled before. Each is experiencing creation as an EXTENSION of the ONE.

Your relationship with your Source then, is completely unique and like no other even though you are ALL equal. REJOICE IN YOUR UNIQUENESS!

This idea is inconceivable to those who are yet in the bondage of the status quo. Your freedom is vast as is your Creator's – for you are one – YOU ARE ONE!

117. THE WORD

The secret teachings of all ages are the words which are given in SILENCE. They are the most sacred of ALL, for they completely EXCEED the physical.

They become LIVING TRUTH for the ones who receive them, and who in turn project them to others who are eagerly awaiting them.

They can never be sold or revealed to any but those who CAN receive them.

They are the words of the ONE to the Son when the two become ONE. They are for ALL, but each must ask with true commitment – BELIEVING he will receive them.

His FAITH will eventually make him WHOLE. The LOGOS, then, becomes the LIGHT OF THE WORLD and is now appearing in every corner.

These words are invisible and inaudible, and their message is indestructible – nor can it be censored. The Great Hall of records will never be destroyed as was the famous library in Alexandria but will continue to convey its TRUTH to the ones who are desperately seeking.

Mystery schools are NOT fables from the musty past, but are REALITY. The WORD was WITH God in the beginning, is NOW AND EVER SHALL BE.

118. EVERYTHING SPEAKS

Everything you behold has a story to relate to you, but you must sincerely desire to know it.

Ask, (believing that you will receive), and it will be revealed to you. But you must listen carefully to what it has to say for it may not always be that which you expect to hear. Everything has its OWN truth. When all is hushed and still, enter quietly into your secret place. From within gaze OUT upon, (and observe very closely), that which you desire to have REVEALED to you. It must be done in complete confidence, in profound peace and without haste.

Observe it in every detail. Imprint its image upon your mind and make it YOURS. Become ONE with it. Never demand, but simply continue to observe and to meditate upon it.

With a little practice, you will begin to receive – entirely without words, a complete understanding which you could discover in NO other way. From that moment, you will POSSESS that which you beheld, and it will be YOURS forever. What is revealed to you will be YOUR secret.

You will never be allowed to put it into words, for they will not be provided for you. In this manner, THE ONE reveals ITS greatest TRUTHS to ITS children. They become yours ALONE and no one else will ever understand them in the same way.

It is the ONE'S secret which IT has shared with you. You will return to your daily life a different being from the one who entered your chamber. Go in God's Great Peace and Love.

119. THE SECRET PATH

"Truth" as REALITY, itself, is far too vast to ever be contained.

At best, it is only possible to perceive GLIMPSES of it from time to time, for it serves many "Masters", each believing it to be HIS – and in a sense, it IS. Each journey through Creation is indeed unique and is interpreted according to previous understanding which always belongs to the PAST; now changed by another opportunity and experience. Sometimes there are connecting points, but at times that can appear to be quite different. It is all continuous growth and change – each affecting the whole and influencing it to some extent. Each new meaning is important to all – but always changing and evolving.

To resist change will eventually retard growth, for one's understanding becomes limited, indeed. This is now a time of unbelievable change and movement. The challenges being presented stagger the imagination and understanding. You must realize, however, that you are most definitely being guided. Seek always WITHIN to find your way through the OUTSIDE world. It is the Secret Path. It is the way of ONE.

TO POINT THE WAY

Kinship with all of being is the mark of the mystic, for well he knows that ALL IS ONE.

He is not called upon to prove it, but only to point the way to those who are moving in this direction. There IS no possible proof for those who know another reality, for this has no EXISTENCE for them. It is not amiss to allow Each to answer his own call. In so doing, he is precisely where he should be, and everything is in perfect order. Answer your OWN calling, then, for it is the one INTENDED for you.

120. THE JOURNEY

It is not without a sense of responsibility that anyone begins his journey to the ONE.

He has heard the call which will begin to change every aspect of his life and lead him to his SOURCE.

It is the journey EACH will eventually make, and which will lead him to REALITY. Once it has begun, the call becomes ever clearer.

Your inner guidance becomes the most important voice you hear and you begin to seek it in every situation which arises, for you realize it will keep you on course, regardless of how important the question may appear to be.

You must remember, however, that it is intended primarily for YOU although it may also be helpful to another. It is your most faithful friend and teacher and is unlimited in the wisdom it can impart.

Make it your constant companion and most sacred contact with the Spiritual realm – for this it IS.

PART X
SPIRITUAL ATTRIBUTES

TOPICS

121. ON GRATITUDE

Gratitude is one of the most positive attributes you can have. It applies to each of you – regardless of your circumstances, for there is none whose life is without much for which they can be grateful.

Real blessings are everywhere in your lives and more are always awaiting the opportunity to appear. Gratitude, as with so many other things in life, is also a form of very positive energy and it is, as you know, energy which produces that which you experience. That is to say that gratitude brings more of the positive INTO your experience.

Make it a daily practice to pause at odd times and to reflect on ANYTHING positive which comes into your mind. On rather ordinary days – one which is seemingly dull and uninspired, if you are willing to open your eyes you will be truly surprised at the many things you have overlooked. Never make the mistake of believing that all blessings come in large boxes. It isn't so.

How often when you are feeling low, a simple comment from another can literally make your day. The reverse is also true – a kind word or a helpful remark from YOU can also help another; and notice how it makes YOU feel.

To have someone call just to say they have been thinking about you is always an encouragement. You are always safe and secure in each moment and anything positive which adds to the experience is a real blessing. Blessings are always there, and they will increase as you look for them and accept them with true gratitude. The most positive of all is that everything grows when energy is directed to it. Try it and see for yourself!

122. RELAXATION

Relaxation is always a good investment.

Most people probably think of it in terms of release and rest after completing a particular task or work, but it is important to REMAIN in a relaxed state while you are working.

Everything goes more smoothly. Your body's responses are more controlled, and you will remain more calm and composed.

Relaxation is not a luxury, but a necessity for good health. One pays dearly for stress in both what he achieves and in his physical state.

It would be ideal – especially at this point, to make relaxation a regular discipline. Your Spiritual attainment would also benefit greatly from it.

Combined with hopeful expectation, relaxation would help provide the ideal state for living in today's world. You must have confidence in the knowing that all is in order and that whatever occurs is for the ultimate benefit of ALL of Creation.

You will be guided all along the way and each will arrive at his destination safe and intact. You can place your full confidence in ALL THAT IS. You have reached a necessary step in your development and all is as it should be.

123. COURAGE

It is truly a courageous soul that forsakes the comforts of today's world and willfully moves out into unknown areas of existence, often in search of what, he knows not.

Many times, the call to do so becomes so overpowering that he can find no peace until he has responded and has set out on his way. This is not necessarily a physical journey, but one which will lead mentally and Spiritually into completely unknown territory. Real growth occurs when one is faced with NEW concepts and beliefs and the complacency which can result from a life without challenges gives way to what will now most certainly be a new adventure. Man would achieve but little growth if he were to remain fast within the familiar.

The lure of adventure has often called out to those who were becoming jaded and bored with their existence. It remains for the brave, however, to create a new path into a relatively uncharted world, for he often has little contact with any who have gone before.

The information and concepts which are being presented TODAY usually mark a true DEPARTURE from the general understanding of the past. You now stand on the very edge of a world which is rapidly disappearing into the past. Many of you realize that you must move on and yet the path is, as yet, unclear. No, courage is not limited to those who have gone on but is now being demanded in an entirely different way.

You should be greatly encouraged in the realization that GOD IS ALL THAT IS. Move on in great peace and love.

124. HONESTY

Seek within not only for wisdom and knowledge of the Spiritual realm, but also to determine if you still have any unfinished lessons or relationships.

Growth occurs on many levels BESIDE the strictly Spiritual, though they are ultimately one. Strive to make your life in every way a CONSCIOUS journey through Creation, for in truth, it is the journey of the CREATOR through ITS Creation.

You are not, nor have you ever been alone, but you abide eternally in the presence of the Source of ALL THAT IS.

IT shares your every thought and sensation and is completely aware of the most intimate aspects of your being. ITS' love is more than sufficient to completely embrace every aspect of your being and to claim you as ITS' own.

You CANNOT be other than honest with the ONE. But why then, is it so difficult to be honest with yourself and with others? REALITY is far, far different from the understanding of the world.

Your call and your challenge then is UNITY. To become ONE again – though you actually are. . . You just do not see it.

125. BEAUTY

When you open yourself to the language of beauty, you are responding to the power of the Spiritual world.

Beauty is always a direct expression of the Spiritual and speaks to man in ways that words never could. Beauty, although it is often expressed in the physical, can lead you into the deepest of Spiritual experiences. It is always beneficial to seek and to cultivate the beautiful. It can be interpreted in many different ways, but they ARE all spiritual – on whatever level. Your sense of beauty will expand as you begin to recognize that GOD IS ALL THAT IS. You will eventually reach the point where there remains nothing which is not an expression of beauty.

Fear will also begin to dissipate with the dawning of this Truth. Everything you encounter is an expression of THE ONE, thus Sacred and beautiful. Contemplate everything you see, meditate on it and relax into its beauty and Truth. Censor NOTHING but continue to seek the Truth and beauty which is to be found in it. It is a wonderful practice to broaden your consciousness. The more you begin to see, the more the so-called negative – the ugly, will begin to disappear and the more the Truth of God will begin to glow all around you.

It will become clear to you that the five senses are also doorways to THE ONE. You need not minimize or fear them – they were God given for this very purpose. ALL THAT IS will speak to you though in ways words cannot express. They are not in conflict with the Spiritual but are points of close contact. They open you to the power of THE ONE. Begin to make this a conscious practice in your daily life. Do not run from it or close yourself off from it. But cultivate it in LOVE.

126. EQUALITY

The structure of your next civilization must be built upon a foundation of true equality – not one of empty words. It will be an equality which truly represents EVERYONE.

Love and respect must form the bond which will hold it together and in place. This new society will not come about through planning and study, but simply through the EXTENDING of true consideration and love to each-and-every being.

It would not be amiss to begin this practice in your life today and in your present world, for the benefit to each would be truly incredible. Its practice will begin a new era of unprecedented growth and achievement which will enrich EVERYONE – not just a select few.

When NO ONE is omitted or denied, the overall growth will contribute to all. Happiness and true joy will abound, and the Spiritual advancement will be amazing.

Rules and regulations can never bring this about, for it can only occur by following the dictates of INNER wisdom. Ironically, it already exists at this time and could become a reality in your present society, but man must begin to see it, to recognize it and to apply it. You are already there, but you do not know it, for the chaos you have created hides it from your sight. The remarkable simplicity of this type of civilization completely evades you because you are seeking that which is still MORE complex.

Truth and beauty abide in complete simplicity, but they will provide the answers you are seeking. Go in Peace and in Love.

127. LIGHTEN UP

You need to lighten your approach and to begin to seek more activity which is joyful and uplifting. It is not enough to theorize about the meaning of life, for life is NOW ...IN THIS MOMENT.

It is far too easy to let it slip by – moment by moment without really living or enjoying it. Happiness and joy are far lighter "burdens" to carry than unhappiness and depression. It is time to reach out to that which brings you real joy and satisfaction and you will find that the Spiritual is there in the midst of it. Even now, your world is filled with beauty and opportunity. Look for it. Know it is there and that it bears your name as distinctly as it does any other.

You ALWAYS have the option to change your outlook and your direction. It can be done far more quickly than you think. There are many around you who would respond to a broad smile and a sincere greeting. Do not let OUTWARD appearances deceive you.

The grey mists of uncertainty and fear have crept quietly in and covered your countryside and your lives. You, yourself, have seen it and recognized it, but it is within your ability to move it out and to open your windows to the sunshine of happiness. You also know this does not depend upon wealth or possessions, but upon acceptance WITHOUT judgment. Another cannot change your reality without YOUR permission, and you are safe, therefore, as you venture out into the beauty of the countryside. You owe this not only to yourself but to others who would benefit from your new outlook. Do not take life too seriously, it is also for your pleasure as well as for your growth. The two are by no means incompatible...but are complementary.

128. HUMOR

Humor is as necessary to a healthy life as sunshine and water. A life without it is much like food without flavor.

The type of humor which is popular at a given time is a good reflection of the emotional state of a people. There are many whose lives are almost completely devoid of humor and some who even believe it is unsophisticated.

The world, however, is FILLED with humor for those who have the eyes to see and the ears to hear. It is truly built into your reality and can speak in countless ways.

Life is intended to be primarily a joyful experience, but man has such a tendency to become too serious. Laughter has a wonderful way of releasing the tension brought about by always looking at the "serious" side of your existence.

Laughter is real music to THE CREATOR'S ears, and IT rejoices when ITS' people are happy and truly alive. Real humor is never destructive but can and does point out so beautifully the foibles of man and the ridiculous extremes he often approaches.

It has been said that even our Creator can "smile" over what might be considered an off colored joke. Keep your eyes and ears open. There is always something humorous to lighten your mind and to keep you from becoming so limited in your emotions and feelings.

Never feel that laughter is unworthy or beneath you, for it is a wonderful gift from ALL THAT IS.

129. WITH A JOYFUL HEART

Approach each day and everything you are called to do, with a joyful heart and your message will be delivered.

The current challenges have only the severity YOU allow them.

Always focus on the INNER meaning and it WILL reveal its truth. You may be confident in your work, for it will affect many.

Accept ONLY the reality which is revealed to you – all else is but illusion.

There are many around you who are there to help, so let not the noise of the outside world alarm you or fill you with fear, but go forth with a joyful heart and in the knowing that ALL IS ONE.

130. WISDOM

Wisdom, as does maturity, comes with time and experience. It must age as does a fine wine. For it too carries the memory of many sunny as well as dark cloudy days, and rain and storms.

It cannot be rushed but must experience the days of the earth. Regret not the clouds and the rain, for they have been necessary for the vital essence of each.

Everything has its place and its moment.

Bask in the sunny days of spring, the fullness of summer, and rejoice in the approaching maturity of autumn, for all is in order – all according to plan.

The vintner well knows how his vines must live in order to produce the essence he desires. Each year is distinct however, as is the harvest, for it carries the stamp of its time.

You may know that it has been a rewarding season, for the grapes are now approaching maturity. Each drop of the wine will show the skill of its creator and his joy will be great.

131. ABUNDANCE

Abundance comes to him who expects to find it. It is the result of living in harmony with ones' inner plan.

Abundance does not necessarily mean great wealth or power, but simply the material means to allow one to pursue his direction without the need of wasting unnecessary energy and time in the process.

It will always be sufficient to enable him to live a truly happy life as long as he remains in accord with his PURPOSE.

True abundance, as wealth, is a state of mind and includes the Spiritual as well as the physical side of life. You will find the truly wealthy in the so-called lower level of society as well as at "important addresses".

You will also find the poverty stricken in the same places. The difference has nothing to do with the cash value of their holdings, but only with their ATTITUDE toward it.

The really-wealthy of the world realize what they have and are unendingly grateful for it. They recognize that it is truly a gift from God and not merely the result of their own efforts.

Wealth, true wealth, belongs to any who can open himself to it and receive it in love and in gratitude. It can never be stored in barns or in banks but flows continuously into joyfully open arms.

The truly wealthy are therefore also humble, though in a different sense of the word. They have found their inner peace and happiness as well as their one true SOURCE.

132. PATIENCE

One of the truly important skills which must be learned along the way is that of patience.

Few there are who cannot improve themselves in this area. Patience is required of each as he approaches the lessons life presents, for without it, there is little likelihood any would remain on the path.

As with most skills, it is necessary for one to realize the NEED to learn it in order to begin.

Your daily world offers every opportunity to enable one to perfect this skill, for lessons are presented at every turn; yet for most, it is one of the truly difficult skills to master.

The real secret to learning patience comes when one finally realizes that he is already living in ETERNITY and that time actually does not exist. Urgency begins to lose its importance and a new order of priorities begins to form.

Peace, peace sublime, begins to override the incessant rush of the outside world and patience makes its appearance – perhaps slowly at first, though surely.

It will eventually become your faithful companion along the way, and you will go in God's Great Peace and Love.

133. THE ONE GOD OF LOVE

Sane and insane, all are searching lovelorn for Him,
in mosque, temple, church, alike
For only God is the One God of Love
And Love calls from all these,
Each one His home.
Sufism

134. WHERE LOVE ABIDES

To walk the paths of love, you must seek the Divine not only in others, but in everything you encounter...for it is there.

Omit nothing from your search, but know it is all ONE and it is the GOD of ALL.

Your own heart, as does all of Creation, weeps each time you withhold recognition, for your innermost being is well-aware of what you are doing.

How could you possibly determine who or what is worthy in the eyes of its Creator? The ONE can only be GLIMPSED in its diversity, otherwise, there can never be any true understanding.

Judgment is not a characteristic of righteousness, but only leads to a divided, fragmented world. Seek the ONE in all things and your fullness of being will know no limits; then you too will dwell where LOVE abides.

135. GOD IS LOVE

How greatly you underestimate the power of your Creator! You repeatedly petition God for Divine assistance and intervention while inwardly doubting the existence of such a power.

God's ways are not to be understood in the light of the general perception of mankind. GOD IS LOVE and that love is ALWAYS manifested within Spiritual law. These laws are immutable and ALWAYS apply. They are never arbitrary or negotiable, but always consistent and JUST, thus they allow God's will to function equally for all.

The perfection of the universe is such that its precision does not permit an arbitrary response as many believe. The most minute action or change affects the whole – it is all ONE. All miracles occur within this framework and the complete understanding can only be grasped within this concept. Of such is a true miracle. It always occurs for the ultimate benefit of ALL, for none are favored, but all are equal in the eyes of God. Well does IT know and love each of you.

ITS truth and mercy endure forever. It is within this understanding that miracles appear – and they ARE indeed miracles. YOU are one of them. Go your way in God's Great Peace and Love.

> God Is Love. And he who abides in love
> abides in God. And God abides in him...
>
> Christianity

136. THE ETERNAL DANCE OF THE ONE

Love comes with the knowing that 'I am that, too'.

It is the ACCEPTANCE of the world around you and not a denial.

The recall and acceptance of the subtle essence of all you have EVER been and experienced, now joyfully recognized and received as a remarkable gift of Eternal Life which your Creator has granted you.

It IS you and is now beginning to speak to you in an entirely different way.

There is no longer anything to be denied or projected onto another, for it BELONGS to life and it is YOUR expression of THE ONE. What was feared and denied can suddenly be witnessed in all its glory, and the serenity of this understanding is beyond description.

It is now UNDERSTOOD that your history of broken rules and commandments was occurring in complete obedience to much higher laws, and the chaos you have battled endlessly was in truth not chaos at all, but the HIGHEST level of Order.

Your enemies have vanished – for they never existed. The simplicity and beauty of Creation are now beheld as the ETERNAL DANCE OF THE ONE – there is no OTHER there.

You may now abide in God's Great Peace and Love. You have only to accept it.

137. ACCEPT YOURSELF

Accept yourself as your truth is revealed to you. It must be with true love and understanding that you go forth into the world.

Words alone will not serve you, for they can be empty, indeed.

Your love for yourself AND your neighbor will know no bounds when you realize and accept who you are.

It has naught to do with piety as the world understands it, but with the TRUTH OF GOD.

What you have done is never so important as who you are, and this – you already know. You have only to accept it as your Divine Truth.

When you truly see it, you WILL see and love your brother as well. You do not have to delay. Ask for guidance from within the depths of your being and you WILL be heard.

Many of you are close – so close. Allow your longing to resound within every cell of your body and it will become so. You ARE being guided. Enter now into God's Great Peace and Love.

138. ON LOVING SELF

In spite of everything you have been told throughout your lives, it is extremely important to love yourself.

You came into the world with this wisdom, but as with so many other things, it has been "educated" out of you. There are those who would benefit by having you see yourselves as unworthy and unlovable.

A child in its natural state would hold itself in complete love and regard and as a result, so very much of the grief and pain of later life could be avoided.

Your sense of compassion comes forth when you can gaze upon another and feel yourself in their place. You can feel their pain, their hurt and their sorrows as well as their love. You recognize in them the same characteristics you see in yourselves and your love automatically extends to embrace them also.

When you do not accept these feelings within yourselves, you could hardly expect to be able do so in another. You, just as they, are sons and daughters of God.

Your holiness is your birthright and because you were born into this life you were born in grace, and you will die in grace – it will never be taken from you; you need never have it granted to you by another. You are always deeply loved, just as is your brother.

True compassion is love in action and it should extend to all of CREATION, for all is alive, all is conscious, and all is sacred. Love is INFINITE as is ALL THAT IS. It knows no limits, it knows no restrictions, and it is never apart from God. God is Love – God is compassion – GOD IS ALL THAT IS.

139. WITHIN YOURSELF

The love you are seeking in others must be found within yourself.

You must COMPLETELY free yourself from all your imagined sins before you can behold the love which abides in others. As we have so often repeated, the outer world is but a reflection of the inner.

God IS love – thus A GODLESS SOCIETY IS ONE WITHOUT LOVE.

When you deny God within yourself OR within another, you ARE denying love. God is INFINITE. How CAN man judge how God speaks to another?

God is equally at home in the daylight AND in the darkness.

It is YOU and NOT the church or temple who forgives man's sins, for they have no existence within THE ONE.

The CHRIST did indeed come to take away the sins of the WORLD. They belong only to religion.

GOD IS ALL THAT IS. GOD IS LOVE. GOD IS ONE. THERE IS NOTHING BUT LOVE. If you are seeing otherwise, you are still remaining in the world of illusion.

Accept THE ONE and you will see ONLY love. IT IS ALL THAT IS.

140. THOUGHTS OF LOVE

We noticed you were thinking about strengthening your ability to love by selecting those who appear to be lovable.

This is commendable but let us point out that those who are most in need of love are often the ones who appear to be the LEAST loveable – and THEY are your challenge.

There are many, indeed, who are truly lovable and reflect it to all who come into contact with them. They stand out amid the crowds.

There are also far too many who are truly starved for love and contact with others but have become difficult to approach. Anger and bitterness replace the love they sought but have never been able to find.

Their reactions to the world and to those around them have become completely negative. You have encountered them many times. Each rejection they experience intensifies their longing and anger, making any contact with them most difficult.

We would suggest you concern your efforts with these individuals when you meet them. GIVE THEM YOUR BLESSING. If they are known to you, begin to encircle them with the pure white light of love when you see them or think of them.

Remember them also in your prayers – it DOES make a difference. They will most likely remain unaware of your efforts, though they will definitely benefit from them. This kind of activity can become especially rewarding to YOU Spiritually, for your own feelings of love will grow in proportion to your sincerity. ALL IS ONE.

Go in God's Great Peace and Love.

141. ON LOVE

Through patience you will know your souls. But it is usually a process which does not occur over night.

Many are the lessons to be learned and many the experiences you will savor and enjoy. Eternal sadness and depression are not intended to be mans' lot, but to grow and expand, coming ever more into loving relationships and experiences. It is not intended to be accomplished alone, but you will grow most along the way at the side of another.

You cannot arbitrarily decide where you will find love until you are well along the way. Love as life itself, has many guises. Only you can know for sure when you are in its presence. It cannot be foreordained by others, by holy writ or by any other rules.

Each time you encounter love along the way, your understanding will grow, and your life will become richer. Each experience brings you closer to the great TRUTH, but it becomes YOURS through experience, patience and tears...yes, tears too.

Love is the meaning of life and it alone will open doors no other key will fit. The power of love exceeds that of any kingdom or force. They will all eventually dissolve and disappear in its wake. Strange, isn't it? Man will so desperately fight this imagined enemy and wallow in blood and wretchedness to escape contact with what he conceives be so weak and ineffective...so lacking in courage and power. Man!

What great secrets and wisdom are so completely veiled, yet even now, right in front of your eyes. The TRUE world – the REAL life, you seldom see at all. You believe it lies in some distant realm accessible, perhaps, to a few who only through the aid of a priest or a saint may find their way!

142. MY HEART IS FILLED WITH LONGING

The love which seems to evade you is crying for your recognition and acceptance. It surrounds you in every guise, shape and manner, but you fail to see it.

It is NOT to be found in worldly goods, but in ALL that is CONSCIOUS.

Love always emanates from the SOURCE, but never from a material manifestation. Open your heart to LIFE and love will abound.

You continue to seek the living among the dead. Let the dead bury the dead, for love is to be found in all that LIVES.

You are now being called upon to OPEN yourself to it, but it is something YOU must do and cannot demand from another.

You have heard many times that God IS love. The Father and the Son are ONE. You ARE love though you still fail to recognize it, but the father's heart is filled with longing.

Seek NOT then, where it is NOT to be found, but go to its SOURCE.

He that loveth not, knoweth not God.
For God is love.
Buddhism

143. YOUR OFFERING TO THE CREATOR

An open mind and a willing heart are perfect tools in the hands of the Creator, for they can respond with precision to ITS will.

In bringing ones' self to this point, you are presenting all that is necessary.

Only true faith can make this possible – THE ONE never requires more. It is only necessary to HOLD one's intent clearly in mind – the rest is up to God.

144. MAKE YOUR WAYS KNOWN

Reach out to those around you to broaden their present understanding. Where there is fear bring LOVE.

Where there is doubt, bring LOVE. Where there is negativity, bring LOVE. LOVE is the meaning of life.

Give MEANING to their lives. God IS love. What better way then, than to bring a "new" concept of God to those who are lost and hurting. It will reach them far more quickly than theological debates.

EVERYONE is starving for love. It is, in truth, the greatest need facing man. The fields are ripe and the workers still too few. Serve wherever you are called, and all will be well. Go forth in God's Great Peace and LOVE.

145. THE TENTH COIN

I require or demand NOTHING of you – neither sacrifice nor burnt offerings.

I demand NO tithes, for this you take as a duty. I am aware of your efforts and I rejoice in your every accomplishment. Your LOVE is my greatest joy. You do not understand the value of your GREATEST gift, for it is WITHOUT price – it is also priceless to me. The most precious gift is given straight from the heart and it becomes a gift to ALL, regardless to whom it was offered. It is the ultimate gift. It is the Tenth Coin – IT IS LOVE.

PART XI
THE SPIRITUAL

TOPICS

Our Knowledge Is Ancient
Ancient Teachings, New Words
Psychic Abilities
On Understanding Spiritual Laws
Fear And Guilt
Open The Gates
Our Worlds Coexist
Connecting With The Spiritual
Reality Or Logic
Where Is It To Be Found
Encounters With The Spiritual
Spiritual Helpers
One
Revelation
Let Your Light Shine
The Secret Society
You Do Not Know Who Is There

146. OUR KNOWLEDGE IS ANCIENT

The knowledge which you are seeking is ancient.

It is being revealed to you at this time as it has always been. It is true for all, and when properly received and followed it will guide all peoples to their goals.

There is no conflict in the message, only in man's receiving and interpreting. It has been twisted often to grant control and power, but that has never been the message we have imparted to you. There is MORE being offered to you at this time because distortions have made our words almost unrecognizable. With more of you receiving our messages, there will be more and clearer understanding, and this is essential at this time.

You may be sure that if the message suggests separation and abuse, war and destruction, they do not come from us. ALL THAT IS, IS LOVE AND CREATIVITY and this is what is intended for ALL. You need never fear our words or intentions, for they proceed from the CHRIST MIND which is quite different from your ideas of Christianity. The results of our words will ALWAYS be Peace, Understanding, and above all else, LOVE, and this will prevail.

The world is NOT divided into two great powers or forces which are in constant competition. THERE IS ONLY ONE PRESENCE AND ONE POWER – ALL IS ONE! When you are seeing a duality, what you are seeing is not in its ENTIRETY – but in a fragmented form. The world becomes whole to you when your sight becomes whole. Regardless of your present interpretation, ALL IS ONE and you are WITHIN it. Make it your practice to seek the whole in everything and in every situation. Your perception and your life will begin to change immediately.

147. ANCIENT TEACHINGS, NEW WORDS

Through you, we are repeating the most ancient texts and are clothing them in new words to speak to a new world.

These texts, some of which are as old as man, bear the same truths they have conveyed since the beginning of time.

They contain the wisdom which has built the greatest of civilizations and united spiritual and intellectual giants with their true Source as well as with their brothers.

Now, the cadenza of this vast symphony is beginning to sound and resound all around you, for you are approaching the climax, which was foretold long, long ago.

The TRUE meanings of life are being revealed.

What was thought to be a dying people is now awakening from its ancient slumber and a vast resurrection has begun.

Think not that God is dead and that all is lost, for you are approaching the greatest Spiritual awakening this world has ever known. Rejoice!

Rejoice greatly that you are here, for you have truly been blessed beyond your understanding. Open your eyes, your ears and especially your hearts to your brothers and sisters who are also coming home. Continue to make your will one with your Source. Your journey has scarcely begun, and your path lies ever before you. Go forth in God!

148. PSYCHIC ABILITIES

The acquisition of psychic abilities is not in itself an indication of Spirituality, although they are closely related.

It is the intent which largely determines the difference.

When you concern yourself sufficiently with psychic matters, you are, in effect, focusing your attention on the Spiritual realm. As we have so often said, you RECEIVE that on which you concentrate. In coming more and more into contact with the Spiritual side of life, you are, then, building or attracting exactly THAT. The difference can sometimes be subtle. When it is done with the desire to help others, the outcome will be far different than for one who is seeking personal power.

Spiritual law, unlike manmade law, cannot be broken. You ALWAYS receive exactly that which you order. Psychic abilities, as we have said, belong to the NORMAL abilities of man. They have been closed off to you by those who do not want you to receive any direct information.

It has been made to look if not evil, then certainly highly suspicious as well as dangerous. That which is brought forth by psychics is usually in contradiction to what the institutions teach. It presents a far different picture than what you have been given to understand. Man cannot be so easily controlled when he is allowed this possibility. As we have repeatedly said, each one of you is different, your lives are different, your truths are different, and your experiences are different. This also, is not accepted by your institutions which have a tendency to place all within the same limited framework. That this does not work is being very clearly shown in today's world. You are indeed free...

149. ON UNDERSTANDING SPIRITUAL LAWS

Such is "the order of daily life", that you must pick up each day at the point where it has brought you.

Needless to say, you cannot arbitrarily regress to a period prior to the origination of a situation or "problem" and redirect your life. For all must follow law – both physical AND Spiritual.

You must approach any issue from the point where you find yourself. However, from that point, it IS possible to apply spiritual laws and understanding to alter the course.

It benefits no one to bemoan the decisions of the past. It is far more productive to focus the energy in resolving the "problem" as it NOW stands.

Such is the case with most of the major situations which now confront you, for you cannot return to the way things used to be.

Man's careless creations must be experienced as well as that which is pleasant and beneficial. It seems so obvious, but as we have said, you never benefit from another's loss. That which you obtain at another's expense will become part of your future lessons. This is always so.

It is not punishment, but Spiritual law and spiritual laws cannot be broken. This fact must be applied in your efforts to resolve these issues. This is not unrealistic dreaming, but Truth. You have within your hands the solutions to your dilemmas, though you do not yet trust them. In addition, many of these "problems" are highly profitable to segments of your society, they feel their success is "locked in".

At this point, a new solution to the world's dilemma is

unlikely, but it will be resolved as each one seeks WITHIN to find his own answer. The artificial borders and boundaries of religion and government must give way to the Truth of brotherhood. Your divisions are neither holy nor realistic.

YOU now stand on the edge of the new world. Others will soon be entering, perhaps slowly at first, but then in ever increasing numbers, and this time is approaching very, very quickly.

You must make every attempt to free yourself from the FALSE restrictions of the past and to open yourselves to the Truth you are seeking. You will recognize it, for it will resonate deep within you. You will KNOW it is the voice of the Christ Mind which knows no separation or hatred. Let Christ, ITSELF speak to you. IT WILL. Go in Peace and Love.

150. FEAR AND GUILT

As the reality of the Spiritual world comes more clearly into focus, you will begin to realize that your lives have also been limited by restrictions the outside world has decreed.

Fear and guilt have not been imposed upon you by your Creator, but by those who wish to control you for their own purposes. Man has relinquished his own true guidance and submitted himself in slavery and serfdom to those who are, in truth, far less capable.

This continues to this day and the arbitrary divisions which have been imposed have separated and fragmented the world as never before. Fear has now brought much of the world to its knees and guilt has twisted men's lives out of balance and inner harmony. These limitations and rules have little to do with the will of your Creator, for you are, in truth, FREE.

That YOUR system of LAWS AND RULES does NOT work is to be seen in EVERY land and race. The only valid laws are those which CANNOT be broken – they are all Spiritual. Real growth can only occur in COMPLETE Freedom and ALL THAT IS, is "wise" enough to know this. There are many, many throughout your world who are also beginning to realize this TRUTH, and the walls of the old structures are beginning to crumble everywhere. Do not be deceived by the loud cries of the leaders; there is a far greater authority beginning to appear in every land. The old borders and rules no longer stand so secure as they once did, and man is searching elsewhere for a new and better way. Do not be misled by the "roles" your brothers have been playing, for the play is approaching its climax. The real battle will not be fought upon a battlefield, but within your CONSCIOUS MIND. Remember...you are completely FREE to go in God!

151. OPEN THE GATES

For countless centuries man has attempted to protect himself by building walls around his cities.

The gates were closed each night and upon receiving word that an enemy was approaching. But which was really MORE important – to keep the invaders out, or the citizens inside?

For the most part, these bastions have vanished with time though in intent they still remain on another level. One which is perhaps even more impenetrable.

But has the real PURPOSE changed? Whatever the REASON, its true origin is FEAR. A fear of the unknown. In your time, man's aggressiveness has managed to penetrate ancient walls the world over and he has brought himself face to face with people of virtually every land and race.

But NOW, which is the enemy?

He is SURE to be there, but you can no longer be certain who he is and your fear has taken on a new dimension. It is, however, too late to CHANGE the reality you must now face.

Can you see the answer? IS there an answer? Could it now really be to build walls around YOURSELVES? This is the impasse you are now facing, but what is the SOURCE of your fear? Is it WITHOUT you or WITHIN you? Only YOU can know this. Go in God's Great Peace and Love.

152. OUR WORLDS COEXIST

We do not exist in another realm apart from you as many of you still believe.

Our reality and world coexist with yours and we are far closer than you might think. For many of you, the "borders" are becoming quite indistinct and your Reality is rapidly expanding.

It is to your advantage to simply allow this to occur at its own pace. Many of the changes are profound and you will be challenged to accept them though they are appearing as the first rays of the morning sun.

You WILL be guided in all things and have naught to fear. Fill your mind with thoughts of THE ONE and you will begin to realize Its TRUTH and POWER.

You have the capability of experiencing that which you most deeply desire to have manifest.

Our words to you are sufficient to see you through. Make them YOURS and hesitate not to share them, for they WILL be requested of you. Ponder them night and day and they WILL become yours.

Move forth in God's Great Peace and Love. We will continue to guide you.

153. CONNECTING WITH THE SPIRITUAL WORLD

Your every effort to contact the Spiritual world strengthens your abilities and your range. The Spiritual world is also ONE, and it is more closely interrelated with the physical than you might think.

There is constant communication, though most of you do not realize or accept it. The soul is Spirit and is immortal. It exists in a realm which is beyond time and space and is most approachable by you in the Eternal Now. Your Creator is present with you as the silent observer. It neither judges nor condemns – but only observes and records your experiences on the skeins of time and Eternity.

Your conscience has been formed mostly by the outside world, and it accurately reflects the attitudes and beliefs of your culture. It becomes an effective tool against you in the hands of those who wish to control and to lead society – in which case, it is manipulated through fear and guilt.

It is still used advantageously today by many different segments of your society beginning with your family, your friends, schools, churches, and the different levels of government. It is wise to examine it very carefully, and it is NOT a violation to do so. Your inner voice will reveal what is true for YOU. It must also be for the ultimate GOOD of all.

This is a process which requires complete honesty, but it will place YOU in control of your life. It can be somewhat difficult to overcome some of its rigidity, but many of its demands simply do not reflect your state of development. This is one of the steps which will lead you to a higher level of consciousness, and it is approaching very rapidly. We have been pointing out to you those areas which require the most attention and work, for they will assist you.

154. REALITY OR LOGIC

Although the vastness of the Spiritual realm is incomprehensible to man, all that is MANIFEST finds its Source and is completely contained therein.

Yet the SPIRITUAL operates entirely without finances or taxes – each being in complete FREEDOM with JUSTICE, but without legal services or armies.

Time has surrendered to the Eternal Now, yet EACH soul continues its unique journey through Creation. Everything interacting on countless levels.

This was all accomplished WITHOUT a random combining of a few chemicals on the bottom of the sea.

REALITY rules in place of human logic which reigns supreme in the physical world; but man still believes that HIS efforts are the source of wisdom and progress.

Man has replaced the Eternal Now with the past and the future. Automatic reactions have eliminated consciousness and man wonders why life has become so confusing and difficult. Many are the eyes which do not see and the ears which do not hear, but the Spirit of the Creator is moving quietly over mans' chaos and REALITY is returning. Sleepers wake, for night is ending.

155. WHERE IS IT TO BE FOUND

"Seek not where it is not to be found". *We have used this phrase many times to bring you to ponder its meaning.*

The outer world is but a REFLECTION of the inner and is never a cause, but only the effect. Regardless of what you behold in your world, it is a manifestation of your INNER state.

The "outer world" is in every sense neutral. It has ONLY the meaning YOU give it.

There are no borders, laws or rules to be found – they exist ONLY within the mind of man. The ONLY means of changing your current world situation is to change your perception.

Trillion-dollar projects achieve nothing for they are not founded in REALITY, but only in illusion as are those differences you behold in your brother.

The fox is still chasing its tail and is amazed that he cannot grasp it. Each time you point a finger, the mirror of the outside world reflects it back to YOU!

You are attempting to override the simplicity of Creation with mental complexities. Sleepers wake, the night is ending! Go then in Great Peace and Love. All is ONE.

156. ENCOUNTERS WITH THE SPIRITUAL

Each encounter you have with the Spiritual world leaves you at a higher level than before.

You believe however, that these events should be spectacular or perhaps, somewhat dramatic. Although this does occur, they are by no means the only valid incidents, (most of which you are unaware). Yet they are REAL.

Your world is not truly apart from the Spiritual, for they intersect on every level. You are assisted and guided at every turn, but you usually do not recognize it.

Blessings in every form flow into your lives and you seldom realize the Source, and the most casual contacts with others are often of REAL importance to you, but they occur without your recognition. You are so accustomed to fragmenting everything that you usually fail to see the WHOLE. Your entire world and everything in it is Sacred. . . as are your experiences.

Those which leave you with feelings of disgust or uneasiness are usually as important to your growth as are angelic encounters. Your losses are as essential as your gains. They are not opposite in terms of good or evil, but simply exercises to give you greater depth of understanding. Strange as it may sound, your world will become more beautiful and exciting as you begin to awaken to the realization of the infinite complexity and wisdom which is presented there.

No, you could hardly say that punishment or damnation are involved – but only Infinite Love and growth. When you finally begin to grasp this profound truth, you will no longer live in fear of failure or of condemnation – they have no existence in the fullness of God's Creation. There is but LOVE. How pale your religious concepts become within this great Light. How FREELY you will then soar!

157. SPIRITUAL HELPERS

There are always those around you who are there for the purpose of assisting any who are seeking the Way.

They are aware of your situations and your problems and help to guide you along the way. You are usually completely unaware of them, for they do not consciously intrude in your lives but aid in far more subtle ways.

As we have so often told you, you are not alone, and you do not plod through life aimlessly or without guidance. These are guides who can be either unseen or visible. They help to bring about circumstances which will lead you to the most beneficial meetings and experiences. It is seldom, indeed, that you ever recognize any of them, yet they are very real and contribute immensely to your Spiritual growth and awakening.

So many of you are highly concerned about "dark forces" which you believe are constantly working to draw you from the path, yet you are slow to accept the TRUTH that there could be positive forces at work.

No, your world is NOT a battleground for a constant struggle between "good and evil", it is, rather, a school for experiencing the results of your choices. You have completely forgotten that life is actually a play and that you have assumed a particular ROLE to enable you to grow in certain areas where growth is needed.

This role has become so real to you that you have completely forgotten your origin and are conscious only of your problems (lessons). Those who are here to assist you do so by helping you to continue to receive GLIMPSES of your TRUE selves. You usually interpret them as fantasies, or perhaps, as dreams. How easily and how completely you have reversed roles and their meanings...

158. ONE

When you truly allow yourself to face the outside world each morning as God's only child, what have you to fear or to shy away from?

This is not a "what if" question, but rather, a statement of TRUTH. It is with this understanding that you will overcome the world.

You have, indeed, inherited richly from your Creator and you have but to recognize it and to accept it as your own TRUTH.

When you come to know who you truly ARE, then who is there to impress? Of what importance is an inflated ego?

The words "To thine own self be True" will be understood in an entirely different Light, for ALL, in the deepest sense of its meaning, will have become ONE.

There remains no OTHER to challenge you or to threaten your position. You will know that you simply ARE and that you are completely unique.

The most profound TRUTH will be revealed to you when you come to realize that you are ONE with your CREATOR.

ALL IS ONLY ONE. GOD IS ALL THAT IS. Go in God's Great Peace and Love.

159. REVELATION

Last night you were visited by angels, but you never knew.

You have often been in the presence of very Spiritual beings, though you were unaware. You are always guarded and guided, but you still deeply long for that which is ALREADY there.

You continue to miss the abiding presence of THE ONE because you are so certain that It will appear in dramatic flashes of lightening or in a great rushing of wind.

You believe that the "appearance" of the Creator MUST occur in such a manner or it could not be TRUE. God does NOT make just OCCASIONAL appearances into your world, for It is INFINITE.

It is, rather, the ABIDING PRESENCE in which you EXIST.

You are never apart from the MOST HIGH. You have only to open your eyes and your ears to behold Its TRUTH.

The day of your enlightenment is drawing nigh, but there will be no great sounding of trumpets or cheering crowds to herald its coming. On that great day, you will simply open your eyes and see...but no one else will be there.

Such is the Kingdom of God.

160. LET YOUR LIGHT SHINE

You can most definitely call unto yourself others who are seeking just as you. They WILL hear and respond.

The possibilities are becoming ever more numerous, for the changes are occurring now. Do not hide your light under a bushel, but let it shine forth, for it will not go unnoticed by those who are seeking.

Make no judgment as to who is acceptable – you could easily be deceived.

But wipe the dust of the past from your feet, this is now a different setting and you should live in great expectation. The opportunities are vast. Dwell, then, in the reality you have CHOSEN as it is indeed YOURS, though you be virtually invisible to many.

Let them be.

Seek in all things that which is the HIGHEST and make it yours – in THIS, there is great abundance and where your HEART is, there shall your treasure be also.

THE GREATEST NEEDS OF MAN ARE SPIRITUAL, and many are starving for the crumbs they are being offered. The harvest is ripe, but the workers are few – you are being called. Go forth in great peace and love.

161. THE SECRET SOCIETY

Each day, you are being given confirmation of the Spiritual growth which is occurring in your world.

The comments which others offer are subtle because they are "feelers" from those who are ALSO seeking. They too are eager to learn of those who are awakening.

These hints are coming from virtually every direction and from many you would consider most unlikely to entertain such thoughts. The most ACTIVITY is NOT always where the loudest noise is pouring forth, for much more is accomplished in the silence of the inner world.

Do not be reluctant to respond, for this will be a confirmation of what THEY are feeling. This is, in truth, the most ancient and powerful of secret societies now coming forth as tiny spots of Light which begin to appear in the morning sky before bursting forth in the beauty and brilliance of dawn.

The last of the dark clouds of night will soon disappear in the overpowering radiance of a beautiful day. The cares and sorrows of the past will vanish, for this day is a new beginning.

Open your eyes and your ears and remain alert, for these clues have hardly begun and yet, their effect is far greater than you can imagine. This IS the approaching change of consciousness many have so long awaited. Rejoice that you have lived to see it, for it is now upon you.

Go forth in God's Great Peace and Love. ALL IS ONE. All is in divine order. AMEN.

162. YOU DO NOT KNOW WHO IS THERE

You behold me countless times each day and you do not recognize me, but I know you and I see you from many perspectives and in many different situations.

Yes, I know you well indeed, and the Silent One WITHIN you recognizes me.

But we pass as ships in the night.

You will never know how many times we could have come together or where our meeting could have led you, but you continue to spend your lifetime searching for kindred spirits.

I call out to you, but you never hear. The noise of your daily world overpowers the sound of my voice.

My eyes search yours for recognition or contact – but there IS none.

Oh! ye who traverse the world in search of Love and understanding, when will you awaken? When will it occur to you to take a closer look around you? You do not know who is there.

> Human beings
> All are as head, arms, trunk, and legs
> Unto one another.
> Hinduism

PART XII
DEATH AND REINCARNATION

163. GHOSTS

You fear the ghosts of the past, but why? Do you not realize by now that they are still living?

Once again, this is a matter of perception. Their experiences do not end with their release from the body, but they move on in OTHER directions. Their presence in YOUR world has as much – or more, to do with YOU than it does with them. They are usually trying to make you aware that they ARE still living, and they have not forgotten you.

The spiritual world is by no means so remote and frightening as you seem to believe, for each of you interacts with it on a regular basis. If you could accept this, your conscious understanding would be far different. Each night, you release yourself from your sleeping body and journey into that vast unknown, but YOU are not unknown there. Your encounters are a NATURAL part of your experiences.

You have blocked your memories because your beliefs and fears have made them unacceptable. Here once again, you are denied the benefits of your own REALITY.

However, you need change ONLY your own perception. Life is meant to be lived, to be experienced. You are intended to grow from these experiences and to expand your conscious understanding.

You still cannot see that EVERYTHING is alive and conscious. All of creation is vibrating in the consciousness which we know as ALL THAT IS. You, too, are a VITAL part of it now and in Eternity. Your journey has barely begun. Open yourself to it and rejoice in it. It is a precious gift.

164. WHO AM I

It is hardly possible to ask a more all-encompassing question,
for your origin is to be found far back in the mists of "time".

Your countenance has been the numberless faces of man. You have had other forms as well. You have lived in many worlds and lands and have indeed, seen many days.

The records you have left are extensive and have much to tell. They are YOURS and yours ALONE and they are unique in creation. And yet, they are the story of man.

You have viewed life with countless eyes and have beheld yourself from virtually every conceivable angle. Though as yet you do not know yourself or recognize yourself completely.

Time, as you know it is becoming short, indeed. If you truly desire to know the answer to this question, you need only to gaze into the eyes of EACH you encounter and experience the resonance which responds within.

THEN, you will know you are VERY close to the answer. Can you accept it?

165. BY THE WATERS OF BABYLON

By the waters of Babylon, I knelt and prayed. Days of toil – back breaking labor. Our wages were labor and more labor and death when we failed.

The days stretched into weeks, then months and years, but this was all that remained. Gone were those who were dear. And gone the life I loved so well.

They said our God had abandoned us because we had not lived up to Its expectations. I knew it was not so, but this is what they said. I could not convince them. I knew God had not abandoned us, for I was still aware of Its Presence – ever urging us to move on. God had not abandoned us, it was we who could no longer hear Its voice, but I knew it was there. Its words still touch my soul and fill my heart with longing. I ache to return to Its courts.

Nothing is forgotten. It is all there – recorded in the halls of eternity. The records you have left, (although each differs in details), all tell of your journeys through time and space. One path is not better than another – they are each unique. Your individual paths have provided each of you with a completely different Truth – a different Reality, for not one is the same as another. One is not true and another false – they are all equally valid and they combine to express the range of my Creativity.

Your contributions are there also, and they provide the details of the OUTLINE which was MY dream. These individual experiences have brought each one of you to the exact point where you find yourselves this very morning. How can you then compare yourselves with another, for YOU DO NOT BEGIN TO KNOW YOURSELVES or from whence you came. There is not ONE other who has traveled your path. Who, then, is to declare what is acceptable to me and what is not?

166. YOUR LIFE AS A REFLECTION

Your lives clearly reflect to you the level of your learning and wisdom as well as your spiritual growth and understanding.

This allows you to experience your attainments in such a manner that they become intimately realized. It is indeed beneficial to examine your present traits and circumstances, for they are clearly visible in your day to day life. Most of you accept them without a second thought, for they seem so normal.

In effect, your lives have presented you with countless clues which have no obvious connection with your background as you understand it.

Your tastes and preferences are often far removed from those of your family or childhood surroundings, yet you do not question them. Your home and furnishings, the food you prefer, your vocation, literature, music, religion, political ideals; your travels and recreational activities often express a far different picture than what you knew as a child.

Many of you have found a mate far from home and are far more closely united than you might ever be with someone from your own town. You accept this without question, but how do you account for it?

It all feels so completely natural to you – and it IS. It could be interesting for you to examine your life carefully through the eyes of a friend or a relative. You might see a completely different picture.

167. THE TRUE HOLY SCRIPTURE

The great library does in fact exist, and each of us is intimately connected with it. Each has access to it by means of INFINITE associations with its contents.

On deeper levels beyond conscious recognition, you EACH consult it frequently in search of the understanding you are seeking, though conscious access to it is within the ability of each.

It is perhaps best understood as a "collective consciousness".

It is vast indeed, for ALL is recorded therein. It is actually the record of THE ONE and the experiencing of Its Creation through EACH of us.

It must be seen and understood from THIS level, for its meaning is not so much personal as it is UNIVERSAL. In effect, it is meaningless without this understanding, for apart from the ENTIRE picture, it is incomplete.

Though it DOES contain the entire record of each soul, its DEEPEST importance is the journey of the CREATOR through CREATION. When seen in this Light, the REAL significance of each individual entity will be seen and understood. Look upon it, however, as THE TRUE HOLY SCRIPTURE.

168. TRACING YOUR ORIGINS

Basic to the understanding of who you are is the knowing and understanding that ALL IS ONE. It is a FUNDAMENTAL Truth which will open many doors.

Many of you are so concerned with tracing your lineage, for you feel it establishes your reality in a world of much uncertainty. You carefully trace your lineage back through many generations to point out the solidity and importance of your family line. You seek out family characteristics and tendencies to verify your character, health and talents, though you carefully edit out that which you JUDGE to be unacceptable.

Strengths and talents are underscored, and all is recorded in your genealogy. You are, however, unaware that you have not one, but TWO distinct "histories". Your family line as you think of it, is actually the breeding stock which provides the physical vehicle you will occupy during each lifetime. It is far different from the relationship of the LIFETIMES which express your SOUL. The physical lineage you claim, is far more limited than is the Spiritual.

Your soul is not restricted to just a few races or continents, but is UNIVERSAL in its expression, for your Creator expresses Itself in DIVERSITY rather than in limited or "exclusive" possibilities. You have probably lived many times in family lines which terminated with your DEATH – there WAS no continuation. In spite of your technology, you still do not begin to comprehend the vastness of ALL THAT IS, or of your own BEING. YOU, as you now exist, represent your OWN "family" line.

Your TRUE family history is the history of your OWN soul and your soul is but an extension of ALL THAT IS. In like manner, your body, as all others, is also from the same Source. ALL IS ONE.

169. REINCARNATION

You search the deepest levels of your memory and imagination longing desperately to find clues to who you might have been in the past.

You are most certain that there is something missing which will complete you or make you whole again. Yes, you sometimes discover suggestions which are persuasive, but you always remain in doubt. The TRUE significance of who you were is to be found in the ETERNAL NOW.

It is the COMPLETE recognition of who you are at this very MOMENT, for you are indeed, the distilled essence of all you have ever been, now viewing your present world through the eyes of EACH life you have lived – ALL focused upon your PRESENT reality.

If the true essence of a single lifetime had been omitted, you would not be the one now seated at your table recording this information. You would, in the deepest sense of its meaning, be ANOTHER being. As we have told you several times, EVERY experience you have ever had was in order and was necessary to bring you to the exact point where you NOW find yourself. This applies also to each lifetime.

They are by no means lost or forgotten but are lovingly included in their entirety within the one who occupies your body. It is the purpose of these discourses to assist you in expanding your state of consciousness to enable you to use the TALENTS and WISDOM within. You are, indeed, free to DRAW upon this vast pool of knowledge, for it DOES belong to you. This is your TRUE inheritance. No, this information is NOT being withheld – rather, it is being opened to you in bringing you to the understanding that you and your brother ARE ONE and that GOD IS ALL THERE IS.

170. MOST ARE STRANGERS TO THEMSELVES

Most of you are and remain virtually complete strangers to yourselves, yet man continues to search the past for the meaning of his life.

It is not to be found in faint memories or in ancient records, but the true meaning is to be found within YOU at this very moment, for it abides within the depths of your present being and understanding.

You sometimes receive brief glimpses in your quieter moments however, these must be examined in the light of your PRESENT understanding and integrity.

First of all be TRUE to yourself and completely honest about what you discover. It is necessary to accept what is THERE and not what you WISH were there. Your truth, as everything in your world, is in a constant state of change as is your understanding.

It is, then, never cast in stone, nor can it be contained within the pages of a book – for it is always ongoing. Thus, the understanding in which you examine your past is ALSO eternally evolving. Is it then, your deeds which give meaning to your life? Do you understand them, or is it something else you are longing to know?

Could this also be found within?

171. YOUR COMPLETE STORY

Why do you concern yourself so with who you have been in other lifetimes, but not so much with who you are at the present?

It is in coming to know yourself NOW, that the "past" will reveal its significance.

The present moment presents the PEAK of your existence as a soul. The sum-total of what your experiences have taught you.

It is the distilled essence of who you REALLY are, and it has quite a lot to tell you about life AND death.

Do you KNOW who you are? Or do you read your story as reflected to you by those around you? Your REALITY is written upon your OWN heart – there is no other source available to you for this information.

It is YOU who must read what is recorded and pass judgment, but you will be assisted by great Spiritual beings who know you well, indeed. The truth therein is YOURS, and you must continue to work with it.

Study it well, for it is also a record of your CREATOR'S view of Creation as beheld through YOUR eyes from the CENTER of the universe. And the Creator has also shared it with YOU.

There is not another story like it in all of Creation.

172. ONE OF YOUR GREATEST GIFTS

Reasoning alone cannot always bring the answers you are seeking.

Very often you do not have conscious access to information you require at a given time, though guidance is always available to you if you OPEN yourself to receive it.

This type of guidance is not bound by the rules of human logic, but often works in ways which completely defy comprehension. In truth, however, it will always produce a sudden recognition WITHIN, and this is your confirmation of its validity.

It would be extremely difficult to function in your world today using only the "acceptable" tools which your education provides you. Fortunately, many of you are beginning to open yourselves to the validity of inner guidance and it is tuning your sight into more Spiritual channels.

The more highly technical man becomes, the greater his need for assistance.

Many have almost completely cut themselves off from the natural world and the beautiful simplicity of life around them and they no longer recognize what IS natural and what is not.

This division has greatly weakened his connection with his Source. Man must once again renew his connection with ALL THAT IS, for many are forgetting who they are. Make every effort to hear, to accept and to take advantage of one of your very greatest gifts, for it is invaluable. It will become a true blessing to all.

173. SOLVING PROBLEMS

When you approach a "problem" in your life and are seeking a solution, you are by no means dealing only with the knowledge you have learned since you were a child, but you are also drawing upon the accumulated knowledge and wisdom you have gained since your "birth" as a soul.

This learning is vast and is always sufficient to carry you through life.

We have also told you that in the course of life, you will be required to come to terms with a situation which finds no solution in the world as you see it.

You are being required to step outside the bounds you have always known and to move on into unfamiliar territory. When this occurs, you are, in effect, moving on to a higher level of consciousness and leaving behind a world which no longer fulfills your needs.

How much more comforting it is to see it as such and to accept it as a sign of GROWTH rather than to bemoan yet another problem. Such situations are truly milestones along the way and should have great meaning to you. When seen from this point of view, solutions of a positive nature are far more easily found than when met with a negative attitude.

The same approach is applicable to both your personal growth as well as to your progress as a people. Your present situation is, in fact, on BOTH levels at this time and the demands you are now facing are great and yet, in each case, you are equipped to solve them if you can bring yourselves to approach them in a positive way without regards for PREVIOUS bounds and limitations. The answers of the past will no longer serve you, for you have moved past their effectiveness. You must be prepared to seek where you have not dared venture before.

174. INNER JOURNEYS

You do not begin to conceive of the amount of information you bring with you into each lifetime.

Your personal history covers a range which far exceeds that which is presented in your schools and for you, it is far more accurate.

When you begin to become aware of it, the apparent discrepancies between your own experiences and that which is taught in your educational systems will begin to bring you to question the validity of your daily world.

This is, in effect, a built-in part of the process of waking up. It is completely in order and will eventually lead you to your enlightenment.

There is, in truth, no subject so "holy" as to be considered exempt from your questioning.

You are, as we have so often repeated to you, completely FREE, though you still have not completely grasped it.

It was never intended that man should remain ignorant of the true nature of life.

As you begin your journey within, you will find that the "acceptable" version of history pales in relation to your OWN Truth – yet they are, remarkably enough, related. You must remember however, that this also applies to everyone else. ALL IS ONE.

Go forth in God's Great Peace and Love.

175. THE LAST ENEMY

It IS a living universe. It is all alive and conscious – though it only exists in THIS moment.

Nothing is held in suspension for the future, but all exists NOW. It is the secret of life and it is Eternal.

All manifestations are NOW. All of creation exists NOW in its COMPLETE expression. There is, in truth, nothing which is dead, for death does not exist.

Death is the last "enemy" to be overcome.

When you begin to grasp these words and to live them, immortality will indeed, be yours. The "Dead" are ALWAYS among the living – your perception must change. LIFE is change – it exists in change.

"Perfection" has naught to do with LIVING but only with life, itself. You have said many times that God is not what most people think, and this is a profound truth.

Traditions and rituals may be beautiful and may provide a feeling of stability, but they are NOT life in its ultimate meaning, for LIFE is VITAL – ever new, ever becoming.

Seek not to remain stagnant but open yourself to life at its fullest. It is your ACCEPTANCE which gives it meaning.

Why seek ye the living among the dead, for you will not find them. . . but the "dead" are, INDEED, among the living. Go His way in Great Peace and Love. He IS among you.

176. A CALL TO REMEMBERANCE

The time of the great awakening is in an important sense a call to remembrance.

As we have said, the veil which descended between man and the Spiritual realm is becoming thin, indeed. As man's experiences begin to increase and grow, he will begin to ask many questions his religions will not comfortably be able to answer.

The Spiritual world is Real. It is REALITY and you will begin to behold it in a new Light.

That which has been hidden will be revealed to those who have eyes to see, as the veil in the temple when it was ripped from top to bottom. The full meaning will finally be understood. Man will know that the last enemy has been overcome and death will be no more. The only mediator between man and his Creator will be the CHRIST who will be seen in ITS TRUE LIGHT. Keep your eyes and ears open and remain in the moment for the LIGHT is now appearing throughout the world. Oh, death where is thy victory – where thy sting? Go forth in God's Great Peace and Love. ALL IS ONE.

177. FOR WE ARE ONE

And silence falls upon the house.
 You feel so terribly alone, though you are not –
 For life goes on for each.
 Your relationship and love have far from ended,
 But will soon reappear as does another day.
 What was gained and treasured will never be lost,
 But will abide as yours forever.
 Then sorrow not that another day has ended;
 Rather – rejoice that it has been,
 For there will be many more.
 Continue your journey ever onward
 And you will meet again and again
 Though the names be different
 As well as the times.
 There will always be a certainty;
 I have known you always
 And I love you more deeply now than ever,
 For we are one.
 WE ARE ONE.

PART XIII
PATHWAYS TO GOD

TOPICS

178. I AM THAT, TOO

GOD IS ALL THAT IS – complete, unbounded Being. It knows no limits, no restrictions, just eternal being and creation... the ETERNAL, experiencing that which IT has created.

IT is free from time, free from space and free from judgment. It is never contained or confined by rules or laws but is eternally free BECAUSE of them.

It is entirely without definition, ever becoming – though never complete.

To the mind of man, the TRUTH of God is outrageous – often immoral – even perverse and evil. IT never abides by man's commandments and laws, but continually presents to man that which is unexplainable as well as unacceptable, then leaves it on man's doorstep for him to contend with.

Saints declare IT is perfection and IT demands the same of man – though man is incapable of this. Others see only satan and the forces of evil everywhere they look – but there IS no true duality.

Sacred writings spread no light to lead the way – but only illuminate that which you are DIRECTED to see. The mystic knows IT is exactly what you CHOOSE to see.

Do You know yet who YOUR God is? You must decide. YOU must decide but TIME is short, indeed.

179. SEEK ME

Seek me early in the morning and seek me in the fullness of the day. I am also here when the sun begins to fade and sink below the horizon...as the stars commence their silent and graceful dance across the dark sky.

Seek me where you might least expect to find me, for I am there also.

This beautiful place you call home is mine as well, for I conceived it within my mind and formed it from the substance of my being.

I abide here also. It is as sacred to me as any temple, for my deepest thought and love went into its creation.

I have blessed you with everything beautiful for your happiness and every possibility you might wish to explore. I have granted you complete freedom to choose whatever you might wish to experience. Why do you limit yourselves so severely?

You fail to see the beauty which surrounds you and you give your freedom away to those who wish to "protect" you. You usually choose the most painful experiences and reject my love as well as that of your brother.

No, it is not fate or some "devil" which is making your life difficult. It is all your OWN choice.

You can learn and grow from the beautiful and joyful opportunities which abound as well. You are not being punished other than by your own choice.

Many of you do not consciously realize that I, too, am here. I am much nearer than you can imagine, and I know your every thought and desire.

You do not see that wherever you walk, you tread a sacred path. Why do you seek that which is incomplete and distorted, but seldom see that which is magnificent and inspiring?

You could change your world of hatred and destruction to the most beautiful paradise – just by changing your MIND. I GRANTED YOU THIS BLESSING AS WELL.

180. AND YET A LITTLE WHILE

Why are you so dismayed to find yourself in a simple cottage instead of a palatial mansion, and that your table is not a horn of plenty as that from which others may feast?

Do you not realize that THE ONE who created your UNIVERSE also dwells therein.

You behold only the outer appearance but are completely oblivious to REALITY. No, you have not been forgotten or pushed aside as unworthy, for you always abide in the midst of THE MOST HIGH.

You, too, are as well known as the ruler who sits upon the throne of authority in your land, though you do not wish to concern yourself with that which you do not understand, but prefer to see yourself as unworthy and rejected.

You refuse to examine that which the OTHERS do not see, for you fear it will not impress them, thus the world of appearances then obliterates the greatest wealth of all.

You pass it by as one without eyes. Your plight is sad indeed, but yours is one of many voices crying in the wilderness – believing yourselves to be punished by a god of wrath and fear.

THE ONE who also abides therein awaits patiently for the day of your awakening from the dream. Sleep well, for your day IS coming.

181. THE PURE IN HEART

You seldom receive so much as a glimpse of what lies within the heart of another.

Your vision is usually distorted by the outer appearance to the extent that you completely fail to behold the incredible nobility and beauty which reside within.

It has naught to do with appearance or refinement, but of an innocence which glows in its purity. Nor is this an innocence which comes from following commandments and rules, but only from a failure to see something OTHER than the Divine in others.

In the midst of daily life, they abide in the Spiritual realm. They clearly hear the words of the Christ who speaks within and His words are, indeed, their Truth. They do not require another to intercede for them, for well do they know God.

Though their days be spent in poverty and toil, their sleep is peaceful and sweet. The morsels they consume taste far richer than the fare of a king's banquet.

Their ways may be childlike, but great is their wisdom. Few indeed, may want to walk in their shoes, but they are, in truth, among the WEALTHEST of men.

No, you NEVER know whom you are judging.

182. A SHORT PRAYER

Someone once uttered a short prayer: "Lord, please help me to become all I am capable of becoming", and because of its sincerity, it was heard, and its response flows on to this very day.

It WILL reach its fulfillment, for it is an ongoing desire.

This prayer was open ended and reflected a strong belief in the future.

One can hardly conceive of the eventual results of such a request, for the changes which it initiated have been vast, and the ones to come will be even MORE remarkable.

What you think of as limitation does not exist in the mind of God and it is also beginning to fade from the minds of those who are awakening.

That simple prayer began a journey which will transcend time and space. Its frequent repetition will ever increase the certainty of its fulfillment and the results will be awesome, indeed.

Consider very deeply and carefully your deepest desire and allow it to become the driving force in your life and you can rest secure in the certainty of its fulfillment.

Go in the great Love and Peace of ALL THAT IS.

183. YOUR PRAYERS ARE ANSWERED

The LIGHT of ITS Love shines upon you each day of your life. Its will is being revealed to you and you are being entrusted to receive it.

It is for all who are WILLING to receive it, and none are excluded.

It becomes open to you when you make a definite COMMITMENT to serve, but this decision may not always remain in your conscious memory though it WAS accepted.

Continue to open yourself, for that which we wish to give must also fit within YOUR reality. You must become as a flexible reed growing by the waters of life and you must realize that you are being swayed and bent by the movement of the Spirit upon the waves.

In such manner, these Truths begin to move into your being, and you will come to respond in complete harmony with this rhythm.

It will become your nature so that you will hardly notice its pulse, but it will be complete. Each time you respond, its rhythm is strengthened, and it becomes more natural to you. It is your DESIRE which opens this possibility to you; we never impose our will on ANYONE, for this would not serve our purpose.

Strive to make YOUR will that of THE ONE, and you WILL be led to Him.

Bring your thoughts to dwell upon that which you long to see, and it will be SO. Have no concern for that which is fading away but open yourself fully to the new world which is now appearing before your eyes. This is the appointed time.

184. THERE IS NO OTHER

Who or what is it that calls your awareness to your inner being?

Was it just a simple decision on your own part or did it begin as the result of a series of hints or promptings?

Perhaps it is not clear to you, but something DID occur which initiated your quest.

We suggest to you that it was the CREATOR, ITSELF which was reaching out to you and you responded. The time must be correct for each soul; it is all according to plan.

You have often been told that this is the appointed time, and many ARE responding. Each is an INDIVIDUAL response to a call – it is not arbitrary.

Everything operates according to law – there is but complete ORDER in Creation. Each and every individual is indeed well known by its Creator who loves it deeply.

This is the Grace you believe must be bestowed upon you by another man though all are completely equal in the eyes of God for everything it beholds is One. There IS no other.

THERE IS NO OTHER.

185. THOSE WHO SEEK THEIR INNER TRUTH

It is often given to them who have been chosen to SENSE it within their being. It is not always given in words, but most often as a vague feeling.

The experiences which will lead them to their awakening, however, may NOT appear to be in keeping with this feeling, but are necessary steps along the way. These people are required to take a closer, deeper look at the nature of REALITY as they experience it.

The usual answers do not fit the questions which are burning within them, and only too well do they know that neither do THEY fit within the structure of their daily world, for there is little growth to be found there.

The discrepancies they find, however, must be sufficient to allow them little peace until they earnestly begin to seek. It may matter little to them if they appear odd or eccentric to others, for their sight is now focused upon ANOTHER reality which is neither understood nor seen by those around them.

Once again, we must repeat the admonition not to judge, for you do not know of whom you are speaking. You never know who is standing next to you or what their purpose might be. Real love can ONLY be unconditional, otherwise it is only familiarity. Real life does not follow a single, carefully detailed plan, but is PRECISELY tailored for each individual.

Your preoccupation should only be concerned with finding your OWN path and setting forth in God's Great Peace and Love. You must answer your OWN call. All that remains is God. God is ALL THAT IS.

186. DOERS OF THE WORD

Endless theorizing about the exact meaning of the Word will never bring you a step closer to REALITY... but will lead you in another direction!

The endless diversity of the Creator renders this a hopeless cause. Your greatest truth is the very one that you deny. That you are FREE. For you too are a creator.

True Creation can only exist in COMPLETE freedom. Your rules and limitations were NOT imposed by your Creator, but by yourselves, (though they have become holy writ in YOUR eyes).

The WORD is not to be found in your understanding of the Scriptures, for it has another meaning. It is the voice of THE ONE as it is spoken to you by the Christ within.

It is given precisely for YOU.

This is the word which is calling for YOUR response. You can only come to God through the Christ WITHIN and this is true for all, regardless of what name it is given. There is always a yet deeper meaning for those who can hear it, for it is INFINITE.

187. TREASURE YOUR MOMENTS IN PRAYER

If you could but realize the value of the quiet moments you spend in prayer and meditation. Your every quest is blessed and your world moves nearer to its TRUTH.

You do not begin to understand the effects of these moments, but they are truly awe inspiring. Far more is accomplished in your chamber than in the halls of authority.

It is one thing to accept what you are doing, but quite another to KNOW it.

Your faith must become sufficient to move mountains, for there are MANY to be moved. You are each being called to become a doer.

Open yourself to the guidance you are receiving in these quiet times – it is your personal contact with THE ONE, and will lead you to your own place in Creation and bring ALL to their goal- whatever it may be.

188. YOU ARE BEAUTY AND TRUTH

If only you could see! You are the Beauty and the Truth which you so desperately seek at every turn. You continue your search ever outward – so sure that you have overlooked it somewhere along the way.

All the while, IT sits quietly within, longing desperately for your recognition and acceptance as you seek ever more distant realms.

You are that expression of ALL THAT IS which has been granted for your OWN understanding. This is not a question of a great ego, but of a simple Truth: you are that part of God which seeks your experience as an aspect of ALL THAT IS. You are Whole and you are True. You are uniquely important to God.

When you open yourself to the life IT has chosen to experience through you, you will have an enormous challenge to achieve, without attempting to understand the paths of others. This is the part of Creation which has been granted to you alone. It is your kingdom and you reign supreme. How much more beautiful and rewarding when you finally come to see and to know who you are. Then, and only then, can you "see" ALL THAT IS.

Your value is inestimable, for without you, Creation would remain unfulfilled. How great the complexity of Creation, how vast – and yet, how simple. The beauty of simplicity lies in its TRUTH. You cannot be other than what your Creator has chosen. You are ITS reflection. Rejoice in this TRUTH, accept it and also accept its Divine purpose. All of Creation is awaiting your awakening to this moment and it too, will move closer to its coronation. Do not seek where it cannot be found but open yourself to the beauty and profundity of the world already within you. It is yours and yours alone. It is as it is intended to be – and it is perfect.

PART XIV
THE WAY OF THE PILGRIM

TOPICS

189. THE PILGRIM

THE PILGRIM
With faltering steps we make our way
Through each day
Seeking, searching, longing
For what, we know not.
Never feeling any belonging
To the world –
To any tribe or clan,
But just an endless longing.
O'er the years
Of trials and tears
We tread our separate ways
Through a haze of timeless days.
And our paths stretch ever on – ever on
'Till eventually we come
To that endless strand of glistening sand.
The setting sun proclaims
Our time has come,
But we have been sustained
By love and a song –
Encouraging words have urged us on.
Now all is peace
And shadows cease casting their spell.
Softly chimes the tolling bell.
All is well,
Yes, all is well.
Yet, there still remain the fading strains
Of that haunting refrain. . .
That ancient, ancient longing.

190. ALL ARE PERFECT IN THE EYES OF GOD

It is a difficult concept for you to accept, but all are perfect in the eyes of God.

Strangely enough, it is man alone who created the divisions and separations and even considers it to have been righteous. Yet, man fully expects that his Creator will forgive him of the very "faults" he condemns in others – though he cannot forgive himself.

Within his innermost being, he does realize the FUTILITY of his situation.

It is for this reason that our words have so much importance at this time, for they will free humanity from the hopeless impasse it has created. They will release him from the duality and from the countless divisions which have separated him from his Creator as well as from his brother.

The world YOU have created is, indeed, illusion and has naught to do with God's truth.

Words of peace, brotherhood, freedom and love are beginning to fall sweetly on the ears of those who are seeking. Pilgrims are beginning to appear from every land and their number is increasing each day.

Words of truth and encouragement will form the new chants and hymns which will resound within your temples.

Let not your heart be weary or your faith be diminished by the falling away of the old. A new LIGHT is beginning to shine upon your world. It is the LIGHT of ALL THAT IS. It is the LIGHT of ONE.

191. THE WAY OF THE PILGRIM

The way of the seeker is not through great halls of Light and perfection, rather along rocky paths of deep seeking and searching.

Nor is the GREATEST wisdom contained in countless volumes of secret learning but is to be found along the by-ways of life.

The true seeker is completely occupied with his search and seldom sees the glitter of the ways of the privileged. His call is ever onward, for the still, small voice beckons him ever deeper into the forests and across the deserts.

Great schools of learning stand silent and dead before him and the small voice is sometimes barely audible – but always there.

The way of the seeker is often solitary and the shadows of approaching night obscure his steps – but onward he must go. He knows that what he has seen has not been the answer and he loses no time amid the crowds.

Such is his path, but he can follow no other. He is being silently led along another route – the way of the pilgrim.

192. PEACE

Think of your mind as a very placid pool. The depths are completely still and without agitation of any kind.

Its calmness soon becomes reflected on the surface and all who approach it are enchanted by its complete serenity. Likewise, shall YOUR tranquility exert its influence on those who come into YOUR presence. Peace, REAL peace, is one of life's greatest treasures and its meaning is DEEPER than the absence of strife and war for it reflects a state of being which is truly difficult to achieve. It is through peace that you will find your closest contact with THE ONE.

Peace, as love, can never be ordained by formal decree, but comes only by INDIVIDUAL behest. It will make its appearance only to the degree it is called. When one ABIDES in true peace, it follows him wherever he goes, never abandoning him or leaving him alone and vulnerable to the conflicts of the outside world. No, it is not the highway of great drama and action, but the pathway of the DEEPEST serenity and joy. It is true, there are countless pathways to God, though NONE is more beautiful than the path of peace. You are now being shown where it begins. Enter in great PEACE and in LOVE.

Shall I tell you
What acts are better
Than fasting, charity and prayers?
Making peace between enemies are such acts;
For enmity and malice tear up the heavenly rewards
By the roots.
Islam

193. ALONG ANOTHER WAY

You have been called to walk this land as a stranger.

Nothing seems familiar, but this has brought much searching and many questions. It is, indeed, the path of the pilgrim who merely passes through, for his search beckons him ever onward.

The glitter of this world has no appeal for him – there is always something missing.

He passes along the crowded ways unseen as a Soul on its nightly journeys until he eventually reaches a small path which leads in another direction.

It is the way WITHIN, and it is here where the familiar begins to return. The stillness becomes music to his ears and its accompaniment is peace.

There seem to be few who find this path, but he knows he is being led on a journey each must eventually take. Well does he know he has been blessed, for there IS another who travels at his side. Go forth, then, in Great Peace and Love. You have found the way.

194. THE PATH OF FREEDOM

Be true to your calling, for what you attract to yourself WILL be correct for you.

If you are true to yourself, you cannot be false to any. The path of freedom is ancient and has been traveled by countless others. It is not the road most traveled, but it leads the way as surely as any other. It requires true courage of conviction to make ones' way in relatively unmarked territory, although the pilgrim is guided and assisted as are all others.

True freedom can only be achieved by granting others the same as that which you allow yourself. You must constantly seek the Divine in ALL. You WILL find it if you are sincere. Lip service is of no avail, for it serves no one.

The path of freedom will always release one from doubts and fear, for they cannot abide together. There remains nothing whatsoever to fear when one discovers that he is indeed, completely FREE. For there are NONE to judge.

This complete freedom grants full expression of the wisdom one has acquired on his journey and his words fall sweetly on the ears of those who can hear them. He knows that his Creator speaks with his lips and that his experiences are, in truth, the will of God. He requires none to grant him approval, forgiveness or a blessing, for he knows he has always possessed them. The world of restriction, rules and fears has no appeal to this pilgrim, and he sees these limits for what they truly are. The call to true freedom is one he can and must answer if his path is to bring him to his true source. The path of freedom is a far cry from the unbridled license which shatters the structure of the old world.

Freedom has no laws because it IS the law.

195. THE NAMELESS ONE

You who are nameless among men, are also a CHILD of THE NAMELESS ONE.

You who have walked the earth countless times in search of the Source of your being and have left no visible records of your journeys. Your toils remain invisible to the eyes of man but are deeply loved by THE ONE who beholds your every thought and deed.

Let not your heart cry out in despair, for you are not alone and forgotten, but you abound in the blessings and eternal grace of the ONE. The meaning of your life is yet held secret in ITS heart but awaits your moment of TRUTH. Your tears are also your Creators', and well IT knows your joys and happiness.

No, your own earthly records do not bear the marks of distinction and honor, but they ARE engraved upon the heart of THE NAMELESS ONE. Strive not to shine where you are unknown but walk in the LIGHT of THE ONE.

Your days are neither lost nor unseen but are the PRIDE of THE ONE who knows you. Let ITS LIGHT continue to guide you and walk ITS path in great peace and love. You, who are nameless, but also eternal.

The noble minded dedicate themselves
To the promotion of peace and happiness of others –
Even those who injure them.
Hinduism

196. THE CONQUEROR

There has never existed a greater conqueror than one who has mastered his own life.

The endless battles and wars of mankind are as naught beside him.

There are no trumpet fanfares to acknowledge such a triumph, but the hosts of heaven stand in silent awe, for it IS the greatest of victories.

The challenges and battles were all fought alone. OTHERS were not held responsible, nor were there any to claim the defeats which were suffered. This victory was not to the disadvantage of others, but ALL of mankind has benefited.

Herein lies its true reward which exceeds by far the plundering of war. It is always a master craftsman who works alone to develop his skills for the good of all.

His name may never appear in history books, though his influence will extend far beyond the borders of his own nation and even contribute greatly to your OWN peace.

He has, indeed, realized his own immortality and continues his path in God's Great Peace and Love.

If one were to conquer in battle
A thousand times a thousand men
He who conquers himself
Is the greatest warrior.
Buddhism

PART XV
THE END OF DUALITY

The Elite
Integration
The Answer
The Whole Is Always Greater
Duality
The Two Are One
The Day Is Ending
The Holy Spirit
The Dream World
The Most Ancient Of Songs

197. THE ELITE

It is indeed a paradox when man attempts to dwell among the elite, for it is, in truth, a world of restriction and limitation.

It is one of the more primitive aspects of society and has naught to do with concepts of the brotherhood of man.

It is far more difficult to strive for universality and unity and this reflects a much higher level of advancement. How much richer and more rewarding it is to abide in the fullness of creation, for one becomes the master of his world – it belongs to him, for it was offered and he accepted it in its ENTIRETY.

There is nothing which was rejected, and his true wealth is beyond measure. Ironically, man does NOT gain by setting himself apart, for he becomes quite limited by his OWN restrictions.

It is only by opening one's self to the incredible range of possibilities and wealth to be found in UNITY that the King's Highway becomes accessible.

All are called to make this journey in great Peace and Love. It is the ROYAL road to Eternity.

198. INTEGRATION

Integration in its deepest sense, can only come about when people begin to recognize and to accept their similarities.

To emphasize differences retards integration, contributing to the DISINTEGRATION of society. The differences between people the world over are not nearly so remarkable as are the similarities. For the inner longings, the hopes and fears, are fundamentally the same. These similarities are more than sufficient to form and bond together a society with incredible unity and purpose. Oddly enough, religion has been a major stumbling block and by and large, has done more to divide and separate man from his brother than any other institution.

But once again, the SIMILARITIES are more than sufficient to bring about unity. It is the lack of understanding of the inner meanings of the words of the Spiritual Giants (and sadly enough, the perversion of their Truths), which have brought about the distrust and hatred which abound today. Any spiritual understanding which does not recognize the unity of all things is not recognizing the works of God.

Regardless of the seeming chaos and misunderstanding which abound, people the world over ARE beginning to hear and to understand that ALL IS ONE. They are the CHILDREN OF THE ONE and are beginning to answer the call of THE ONE who dwells WITHIN. Their number has been growing silently, but ever so rapidly and they are creating a new world of peace and love. The word "integration" is taking on a new meaning and understanding today, for it is not based upon illusion, but upon the Truth each one hears and knows WITHIN. Go forth in God's Great Peace and Love. ALL IS ONE.

199. THE ANSWER

Waves from the ripples you have created in the past are now beginning to wash upon your own shores. They have grown in intensity as EACH has contributed to their energy.

It is best, perhaps, to think of the gathering storm as a cleansing and release from the negativity you have allowed to form, for it will wash away the pollution which has distorted your vision and poisoned your minds and bodies. In truth, not one can point a finger at another, for each in his own way has influenced the situation. As long as you hold to the narrow and mistaken belief that it is THE OTHER, who must come to YOUR point of view before your problems can be resolved, you are not seeing the reality of God's Truth.

It is NOT up to you to define your brother's place in Creation, for you have truly never found your own. You never consider the POSSIBILITY that another's understanding could have some validity, for it is not in complete agreement with your own. Most of you, however, never bother to examine the VALIDITY of your own beliefs. You accept what you have been given as truth, thus, your own position is in NO way different from that of any of your brothers.

There IS no one truth. Your way is NOT necessarily better than your neighbor's, nor is his way intended for you, although your ultimate destinations are the same. Nor are you in a position to determine with any degree of accuracy, the level of your OWN spiritual development. Your only possibility of changing and improving your world lies in changing your own PERCEPTION. This is within your own hands and YOUR world can be completely healed in this process. Your success in this effort will depend entirely upon the SINCERITY of your desire to make the world a better place.

200. THE WHOLE IS ALWAYS GREATER

At first, many of these new ideas will seem strange indeed, for they are so vastly different from your former concepts.

You will find, however, that when you begin to put them into practice, the results will be highly rewarding. For they are in harmony with both natural as well as Spiritual laws. Basically, they are not conceived to place any species in a disadvantaged position, for everything works together as a whole which exceeds the sum of its components. At any point where a segment is hindered in its free development all of creation, in a sense, suffers for ALL IS ONE.

The ripples are felt everywhere. Man only deceives himself when he seeks to gain at another's loss, for it WILL become HIS also. The harmony and balance of creation are wonderous, for the energy which is released by its unimpeded functioning radiates throughout the universe.

Yes, the interconnection of all things is completely beyond comprehension – there is absolutely nothing which is ultimately apart from it. The whole is always greater than the sum of its parts and this concept is vital to the resolution of your current problems.

The affirmation that GOD IS ALL THAT IS, is true at EVERY level – there are NO exceptions. Free will automatically grants you the experience of your choice. The weight of your choice also falls on the shoulders of others and influences their experiences as well.

As we have so often said, you form your creation initially on the MENTAL level. The energy which is fed into it can be shared by any who also contribute to it. To the extent they do so, they become participants in that creation. Nothing comes into your experience unbidden.

The same laws which bond you, also serve to RELEASE you from it. This is the magic key which will move you through the upcoming changes. The repetition that ALL IS ONE is by no means a shallow phrase of a group of radical individuals, but a great Spiritual Truth.

This should be repeated by all who wish to progress in their spiritual development to the next phase which will result in a new world. The interconnection of all things is beyond your complete grasp, though its truth will be experienced by every level of your existence. Spiritual laws cannot be broken, and they are ETERNAL.

201. DUALITY

It is long and difficult indeed, to take the path of opposites through creation.

The world of fragmentation offers little to point the way which remains ever divided and unclear. Neither TRUTH nor REALITY can be seen or grasped apart from its wholeness. Anything LIVING is far different from its inert form. Nothing is truly itself apart from its completeness.

Why seek you always the living among the DEAD?

The complete manifestation of the Creator is Eternal Life – fullness of being. You are attempting to breathe life into a corpse which YOU have slain and dissected in your curiosity – but it remains ever a corpse.

You are failing to grasp that THE ULTIMATE REALITY IS SPIRITUAL.

It is this which makes the whole MORE than the sum of its parts.

You continue to attempt to solve your "problems" by working only with DEAD facts. Nor can you ever force a solution in this manner. It is not possible to force a solution which is spiritual, you must ALLOW it to manifest according to its own laws.

The wise are beginning to grasp the ILLUSION of duality and its hopelessness. Time, as you know it, is short, indeed. You are free to continue as you have or to accept that ALL IS ONE.

Seek your way in God's Great Peace and Love.

202. THE TWO ARE ONE

All is ONE. The pathway which unites AND the one which divides, are but two manifestations of the ONE.

That which continues to divide is leading to further experience on the physical stage, while that which unites is preparing others to move on into Spiritual life.

The current change in consciousness will also affect the EXPERIENCE of the physical world. All is in order. Each is realizing the results of his choices and will continue to grow.

Nothing is lost – each will find his way.

The STAGE of the world will no longer continue to have any reality to those who are moving on, just as the Spiritual realm has little meaning to those who are still learning the lessons of the physical world.

Do not, then, become dismayed by the apparent conflict, for it is, in truth, all but ONE.

You will continue to receive confirmation of the changes everywhere you turn – they are real, and they continue to accelerate. Your brothers are among you in far greater number than you can imagine. Each will be guided to his OWN truth. ALL are being called to go forth in HIS Great Peace and Love. ALL IS ONE.

203. THE DAY IS ENDING

The pages are falling from your calendar as leaves from a tree in late autumn.

The rays of the early morning sun have already faded into the pinks and purples of twilight and man draws nearer to the appointed time.

Have your science and technology provided you the understanding that is now being required to see you through – or perhaps your philosophy or religion?

For far too many they have all fallen short. Their answers are no longer so clear in the haze of sunset as they were in the bright Light of mid-day. And yet, your world knows all too well that the day is ending.

What if you have not really grasped the meaning of life?

Could there, in truth, be another answer?

Where can you go?

Where can you seek?

It is late, indeed, but you DO know the answer. It is engraved upon your HEART. You must go within. . . WITHIN.

204. THE DREAM WORLD

When the sun fades into the evening shadows and the natural world is hushed and still, the Spiritual world remains active.

Much is accomplished in the shades of night and the activities of the past day are digested and acted upon.

You are strengthened and nourished and the rest your body requires also contributes to your "rebirth" into the next day, but the soul takes leave of the bonds of the flesh and goes about its work in countless ways.

Most of what you experience begins to fade away with the approaching dawn, though it has served its purpose.

You are often left with puzzling memories in the dreams you can recall, and you attempt to read them in terms of your waking understanding – though they usually remain strangely mysterious.

They do, however, make you aware that there is far more to your life than you know. It reminds you that there is, indeed, ANOTHER world and that you are also active in it.

The people that you meet and know there are REAL people, yet in your waking state, you know them not... Who are they? Do you ever see yourself? Do you know WHO you are? These people, places and events present you with other aspects of your life which are now unfamiliar to you – and yet they are real. They do, in fact, EXIST and strangely enough, the meanings are important to you and DO have significance in your daily world. In your dreams, you are FREE – you are not restricted by the physical and you can move about as you wish. In the simplest of terms, this is a reminder that you ARE FREE.

You are not limited to the small world of your daily life but are completely free to explore countless paths which are open to you, but which you usually do not see.

They do exist, none the less.

It is through combining the flexibility you encounter in your dreams with the clarity of your daily life that you will become adept in moving forth in new directions. They are there, and they are yours to travel and to explore.

They are a part of Creation and offer many new opportunities. You are not limited except by your unwillingness to look more closely around you. There are countless hints being given you daily, though you usually do not perceive them nor, are the answers you are seeking limited to your so-called "real" world.

Study your dream life carefully. It has much to relate to you and can lead you in directions you do not now imagine. Watch for those you see in your dreams you might encounter them when you least expect it. Your world is changing very quickly, and you are also changing. Be alert to everything around you. You will be amazed at what is happening. You, too, are a part of it. Make it yours also, for IT IS ALL ONE.

205. THE HOLY SPIRIT

It is the active Will of GOD as REFLECTED through THE CHRIST. It was brought to the awareness as the Holy Comforter and still must be awakened within each.

It empowers each soul which comes to the awareness that it has DIRECT access to God without an intermediary. You may think of it as the INNER VOICE.

The Son of GOD was given this gift thus it abides within EACH. Blessed is each who recognizes it and RESPONDS to its word, for he is, in truth GOD'S ONLY SON. This is the purpose of going within. It is to be found within THE TEMPLE OF THE ABIDING PRESENCE and it is THERE where you will find that which you are seeking and NOT in the outer world.

Question: How can I welcome the HOLY SPIRIT?

Response: COME HOLY SPIRIT

Come Holy Spirit
Make my heart your home,
Abide with me now and evermore.
Let my thoughts be Yours
And grant that Your words
May fall from my lips and touch others
with the intensity they affect me.
How grateful I am
For Your presence in our lives.
Help me to become worthy,
Help me to become Yours.   Amen.

206. THE MOST ANCIENT OF SONGS

That most ancient of songs is once again being heard in your world, though its words had been forgotten by man.

The melody is as old as creation and the words have echoed down the halls of time, itself. They have been heard and repeated in every land and era, but they have always become confused and forgotten by a world which has so often preferred to march to another drummer.

The battles which have so often isolated and destroyed mankind and have left the earth scarred and desolate always bear solemn witness to the TRUE path of the drummer. Once again, man begins to ache for the quieter strains and noble words of that most ancient of refrains.

Mystics and sages the world over have guarded and continued to repeat the sacred texts to a world which all to quickly begins to alter the words for its own purpose.

Those perceptive souls who have remembered these sacred themes and the subtle music eventually begin to grasp their true meaning and to turn away from the crowds. Man is once again beginning to awaken to the REALITY he has forgotten.

As the wise ones recorded so long ago, this is the time of the GREAT awakening and now, ever so gently over the incessant beating of drums and the crash of cymbals, a counter theme – a descant of the most haunting beauty and TRUTH is beginning to fall on the ears of a weary world It is the music of the spheres – the Song of Destiny.

PART XVI
CONSCIOUS EVOLUTION

207. UNITY

Make every effort to move quickly into the unity of life, for you now stand at the threshold.

You are now beginning to feel the Truth of the words we have been giving to you. It is indeed, a world of UNITY and the concept of duality is beginning to fade from your sight.

Strive diligently to see EVERYTHING in its completeness of being and the shattered world you have known so long will be replaced with a beauty you never realized was there.

Be not deceived by the last vestiges of duality but bid them leave you in peace and joy.

Do not allow your old image of the world to accompany you any longer, rather open your eyes and your ears ever wider to the TRUTH of Creation. Make no attempt to limit the new, for as yet, you cannot imagine its fullness of being.

Begin today to walk a new path into a new world. We are with you.

208. INVITE THIS DAY

It is only within YOUR heart that duality is resolved, and all becomes ONE.

YOU are the god of your universe and you DO reign supreme. But your obligation is only that which falls within YOUR jurisdiction. Your influence will indeed be felt throughout creation, but this is your only responsibility. Your universe moves through creation according to law and at the behest of the Creator – yet it is ONE.

Make YOUR will one with that of the Creator and ALL will become ONE.

Invite, then, THIS day the wisdom you need most at this point and it will be provided.

209. FINDING PEACE

Peace be unto you who today seek peace.

It is not a gift as such, but the result of victory over countless battles through time.

Real peace is far deeper than just freedom from war. It comes as a result of the complete acceptance of life, just as it is, and with true participation in it. Peace can never come in its entirety to those who insist on living in a FRAGMENTED world. It can be grasped only by those who see far beyond a blind resistance to REALITY.

The message from our side to you for some time has been a wakeup call. The hour is drawing nigh for your decision which will determine your next world. We have been repeating that YOU form your realty – that you will experience the life you are now creating.

There are many of us who are speaking to you and many of you who are beginning to listen. Do not entertain thoughts of a life which does not appeal to you but bring your thinking to bear upon the highest perfection you can conceive, for it WILL become your experience.

Dare to look at all as ONE. EVERYONE and EVERYTHING has its place whether you see it or not. Each time you broaden your view, the less negative your life will become. In effect, war and destruction are not thrust upon you by some "evil" OUTSIDE force but are the result of your thoughts. You REMOVE yourselves from conflict by not INVITING it through your THINKING. There is a world of peace and beauty awaiting you. It is already there for you if you are ready to accept it on ITs terms. You must love ALL THAT IS, you must love your neighbor and you must love yourself – just as you are. Then, you will find Peace Profound.

210. PEACE WILL COME

Peace WILL come, but ONLY at YOUR bidding.

It is something each must truly desire, for lip service alone is ineffective. True peace is inevitable if you really seek it, then it will enter softly and unannounced into your being as does the awareness of the Christ. You can neither command nor force it in any way, for it appears only when YOU have prepared the way. Real peace is not a mass event, but as does enlightenment, comes to each INDIVIDUALLY when the call is great. It can indeed, appear to be worldwide as will be the approaching change. Regardless of the name you give it, IT IS THE COMING OF THE CHRIST. ITS flock will be one people and one truth...ONE !

THERE IS NOTHING OTHER THAN GOD

Your entire world is but a reflection of the mind of God in any given moment.

It is never still but is in continuous change and creation. You, as an aspect of God are always present in this activity, and it is Eternal. You are never, nor can you ever be APART from God, for GOD IS ONE. You, just as the Father, are what you CHOOSE to see in any given moment. You are responsible for your creations. CLAIM them. You will experience them on every level, for it is not possible to run away from yourself – you are ALWAYS present. You, as the Father ARE Eternal, but your world of illusion is about to end and many of you are coming to realize who you are. Open yourself to these changes and rejoice, for you are returning to REALITY. There IS no duality. ALL IS ONE. THERE IS NOTHING BUT GOD.

211. E. PLURIBUS UNUM

It follows that when you make your thoughts ONE, your life will also become ONE.

This is the mysterious secret of harmony and health. It accomplishes little to approach each disharmony as a single issue, for the answer is always found in UNITY.

All disharmony, all unhappiness, war and disease result from being out of harmony with ones' purpose – thus with life itself. This by no means implies that each must lead identical lives, for creation itself, is expressed in diversity.

You will come into harmony AUTOMATICALLY when you become true to yourself.

You cannot, in truth, override your inner direction, for this resistance results in negativity. It is the spirit of wisdom which brings you to listen to your guidance.

Health is a major issue today, for man has become so far removed from his purpose in life. The normal approach to his "problems", is to attempt to remove the manifestation while failing to confront the cause. It is a futile approach and is resulting in much suffering and expense. Regardless of the problem, the answer is always to be found in ONE.

Your only true understanding of this can come from within. It is difficult to intellectualize it, for the answer of necessity, is different for each.

Simply put, when you become one with your individual purpose, you will automatically come into complete harmony with ALL. GOD IS ALL THAT IS.

ALL IS ONE.

212. HEALING IN YOUR WORLD TODAY

Healing abounds in your world – even today.

Most of you, however, have placed it into the hands of those outside you. You have relegated your own abilities and strengths to those whose true interests lie in other directions.

Healing and wholeness are the natural responses to your own inner desires and outlook and cannot be contained within or presented to you in a pill bottle. Health always depends upon your own deepest desires to become and to remain WHOLE.

Why do you wonder that you feel so cut off from life when your response is usually to grant to others the RESPONSIBILITY which is yours alone! Healing comes with your sense of FREEDOM – of knowing that you are in HARMONY with life – with ALL THAT IS.

The discourses we have been presenting to you are for this purpose. Health belongs to those who have healthy outlooks toward life. It cannot prevail where there are always thoughts of limitation, judgment, hatred and fear.

Health responds to a peaceful mind which has embraced life in its TOTALITY. You must ALLOW healing as well as forgiveness, compassion and love. The most expensive treatments avail you nothing where there is no will to live. The body responds to and reflects your deepest desires as the surface of a calm pool does its surroundings. Do not continue to deceive yourselves. Reclaim your birthright and watch your inner peace and health begin to return as does the sun on each beautiful day. The responsibility for your health does not lie in the hands of the outside world, but within YOURSELF. It is you alone, who chooses to be well or to become ill. Think about it.

213. YOUR SINS ARE A MISPERCEPTION

The healing of that which you assume to be unacceptable is in no wise different from the healing of that which truly IS.

All healing is, then, your release from the feeling that something in your life is not acceptable.

These feelings do not originate in God, but only from your misperception. All illness comes as a result of your feeling that you must be "forgiven" for something of which you are actually innocent.

As we have so often said, you have been granted FREE WILL, but in order for you to learn the results of your choices, you are allowed to experience how these actually affect others as well as yourself.

There is never any punishment involved, only learning and growth. When you once accept the infinite wisdom and power of God, you will realize that you are completely FREE and that your "sins", in fact, NEVER EXISTED.

If you are whole, your body can no longer reflect illness, for you will see that it was TRULY a misperception. You are all, each-and-every-one, children of THE ONE.

You are ITS extension into physical form and thus, you are also Spiritual beings. When you awaken to your true identity, all illusion will disappear. Time and separation will vanish and you will know who you were from the start. Arise!

And walk. Go in great peace and love. ALL IS ONE.

214. SOUL GROWTH

Just as you know that you can expect the dawn and dusk of each day and the passing of each season, you must also come to know that there are definite "seasons" in the cycles of life.

They do, however, bear more significance than you might think.

They reflect not only definite periods of development of the physical body, but also apply to soul development as well. These Spiritual aspects are not so firmly established in TIME as are those of physical life, for they are far more complex and are influenced by many more factors.

When seen from a more extended point of view, they fall more clearly into patterns or cycles. It is very easy to misinterpret them by simply viewing them as MORAL development thus either positive or negative, but this is far from an accurate picture.

What you think of as SPIRITUAL growth is not limited to a single lifetime experience but has its origin within the Creator, Itself. Its course is INFINITE and thorough.

As we have been suggesting to you, it is a process whereby the Creator is able to experience ITS own dreams of creation through each of us. We are, then, actual EXTENSIONS of God, so formed that in our TOTALITY we share every aspect of ITS creation, which proceeds from the infinitely small to its ultimate extension – INFINITY, itself.

What usually appears to be CHAOS, however, follows definite LAWS and everything progresses in an orderly manner. This can only be observed from a remote and highly magnified point of view. The more condensed each segment becomes, the less "apparent" it seems to be. That which you view as soul growth when seen as a lifetime experience is, then, highly distorted, for it is truly far more vast.

215. FOR YOU ALONE

We cannot stress enough the importance of the inner world. It is the SOURCE of everything manifest, for nothing exists apart from it.

Whatever you seek has its REALITY only within. This applies also to ALL healing. You will ALWAYS come out short when you seek the Source in MANIFESTATION.

By and large, the scientific community does NOT recognize the Source, but ONLY the manifestation.

Your inner contact with your Source is DIRECT. It will supply all your needs and you will always be guided. You are each unique, thus your REALITY is also distinct.

It is custom made for you alone and not something which is to occur TOMORROW, but which exists at this moment in its complete fullness of being. Accept it and move into Eternal Life. It is the long expected and awaited change of consciousness.

216. SPIRITUAL LAW

There is often much talk about miracles, but many people do not understand them. Miracles do indeed exist and can happen quite frequently.

The chaotic situation in which man now finds himself, quite easily brings his thoughts to entertain the POSSIBIITY of miracles. It is quite easy to distinguish between them and fantasy, for true miracles never require the overriding of spiritual laws which, as we have said, are immutable and can never be broken.

Miracles always occur within those aspects of creation which are flexible, and which are subject to probability. These include the realms of time and space, for they are never fixed as man believes, but are truly malleable.

Thought forms also provide many examples of what are often termed miracles for they can give every indication of being what they are reported to be – and in a sense, they ARE.

Very deep desires and beliefs can and do bring about these events which also follow spiritual law for you DO experience that upon which you concentrate. These areas, then, provide the background for all true miracles, some of which can be impressive, indeed.

When you now reflect upon some of the famous events of which you have heard with this understanding, you will receive a different picture of the unseen world. The differences are sometimes subtle. You must remember that you live in a world of UNLIMITED possibilities, but it always functions within given laws. These laws are never set aside, for there would remain only chaos – but even chaos itself, operates according to law.

217. THE TIME OF MIRACLES

And again, we tell you: they are MORE than sufficient in number in your land to change its course.

You are living in the time of miracles and they abound all around you. Expect them and open your heart to them, for they are Real.

Speak words of encouragement and they will be eagerly accepted, for you have nothing to fear if you do not invite it.

You are having difficulty in recognizing your brother AND the CHRIST, for he is EACH one you encounter. Release yourself from the burden of judgment and starting with YOURSELF, go forth in HIS great peace and love. . . you are coming home.

If YOU love and serve the God of YOUR heart, all will be in order for you, AND your brother. Rejoice and open your heart to each, for you ARE ONE !

218. ONLY YOU ARE RESPONSIBLE

It is not our intention to deliver pages of startling predictions or dire warnings. They will not accomplish what we are striving to do.

It is our desire to awaken you to the fact that it is YOU who is responsible for your future – not some president or military figure – but YOU, yourself.

You accept or reject all possibilities with the thoughts you entertain each and every day. It matters little what the outside world is doing, unless their thoughts are ACCEPTED by you.

This, in truth, is where your REAL vote is cast.

Do not deceive yourselves by feeling that it is your duty to go along with mad schemes which will lead to death and destruction. You completely underestimate the power of your TRUE vote, for it can never be recast or lost in the counting.

You DO cast a vote each and every day with your THOUGHTS and DECISIONS and it is this, and this alone which determines your future.

Wake up! The alarm is sounding.

A new day and a new world is appearing and you can make it yours through your acceptance of the TRUTH we have been pouring forth into your world. Examine very closely your inner response to what we have been repeating to you. It will reveal your destiny far more clearly than any outside authority. It is your choice. You may go in God's Great Peace – or march to another drummer. GOD IS ALL THAT IS.

219. THE PLAY

To release oneself from the illusion of the "play of life" is perhaps, not such an easy task. The first step is in the realization that it is actually just that – an illusion.

Your true life is on the other side and man is here on the earth stage for such a very short length of time in each incarnation. In periods of real spiritual growth, the lessons become more intense.

When you eventually reach the point where you realize that you have been through a situation countless times you begin to long to move on. This is most often an INDIVIDUAL decision. You begin to see this in the vanity and hopelessness of your attempts to judge others and their actions. The slightest effort to do so can pull you right back into the action and you become an unwitting actor in ANOTHER round.

You also begin to recognize the familiarity of the actions you are judging and often the sting of their consequences remains fresh in your subconscious mind. Separation, isolation and loneliness also eventually come to be very unappealing, and you ache for love and acceptance.

When the desire to remove oneself from the stage becomes strong enough, you may remember that many of the dramatic scenes actually had NO satisfactory answers on that stage and in order to move on, you must seek a higher level.

When this realization occurs in large numbers of people, a new era is about to appear and there can be a conscious leap into another reality. This also occurs through widespread disillusionment and depression. The seeds were sown long ago, the crops have grown and matured, and the harvest is now ripe. It will be a time of great rejoicing when all are gathered safely in.

220. THE PLAY IS ENDING

Make your decision this day to take your last step out of the outside world of fear, guilt and turmoil into the emerging world of Love, Unity and Peace.

There is little more to be gained by endlessly debating the hopelessness of your world conditions. The devolution is well in progress and it would be wise indeed to completely release yourself from the negativity which abounds.

Move into the NEW in thought, word and deed and it will very quickly become your REALITY.

Do not attempt to return to retrieve MATERIAL possessions which will all to soon have little, if any value.

Seek your brother in EVERYONE you encounter and only RECOGNIZE him as such. The Christ is everywhere you look and will make Himself known to those who are seeking.

The kingdom is WITHIN and not to be found in the world of illusion. The play is ending – it is time to come home.

221. THE SOLUTION IS NEAR

It is most important to remember that your "world crisis" HAS no reality other than within the mind of MAN.

There is not a single "problem" connected with it which could NOT be resolved by the simple act of changing your perception.

It is a highly dramatic ILLUSION which has evolved from guilt, fear and projection. It has nothing to do with man's being punished by God but only with his failure to understand the REALITY of creation.

Each day in this direction leads the participants of this drama further away from the peace they are seeking. There are MANY among you who are beginning to see through this illusion and who are seeing a far different Reality.

Many are beginning to find their brothers all over the world and to remember the true Christ which is now being seen in every land and nation and the LIGHT of this truth is overcoming the darkness of fear and projection.

The REALITY of Creation is the Infinite Reality of its CREATOR and not the results of man's efforts. Rejoice that it is so, for there IS an answer forthcoming and you are very CLOSE to it – IT is WITHIN you.

Go then, in Great Peace and Love.

222. A TIME OF OPPORTUNITIES

When you have learned to FUNCTION consciously on more than one level, you will have reached the point where true Spiritual development can begin.

This same ability allows man to begin to function on OTHER planes as well.

The actual REALITY of your being far exceeds that which is familiar to you and the more Spiritual aspects can then begin to be understood in a new Light.

This ability will offer man new hope in a world that APPEARS to be in a hopeless situation.

Your possibilities exceed by FAR those which your personal understanding allows. These abilities are beginning to appear now in your world and the upcoming changes will soon move mankind into another realm.

Begin to open yourself to the meaning of these changes, for you will be deeply affected by them. Go now in Peace.

223. SHADOWS OF THE PAST

When one truly abides in the Eternal Now, the shadows of the past disappear INTO the night which has passed and the morning sun, bathes the world in the LIGHT of a new day.

The warmth and clarity of day show forth the beauty you could no longer see, for what you behold appears as a NEW creation – and in a sense, it is just that.

The lifetimes of endless repetitions of the play have dulled your vision and hidden the REAL world from your sight. This new day is now dawning very quickly, and the drama of the past is quickly giving way to the reality of Peace and Love.

As we continue to repeat to you, you must ALLOW them to become yours.

Walk gladly into the new and let your heart rejoice in your victory. It began with the TRUE desire to know your Source – the FIRST step of this journey through time and space.

You have, indeed, been greatly blessed to be here at this time.

224. YOUR HIGHEST SERVICE

It must be your own decision to remove yourself from the drama of the outside world, and your intent will suffice to break the bonds which have held you captive.

You can most definitely be of higher service to others by means of your OWN Spiritual growth.

As we have so often said, the continuation of the actions of the past cannot possibly offer a solution to the current situation of your world. It is only in seeking a HIGHER level of understanding that your challenges will be understood for what they are.

Each individual who contributes to this greater understanding will be offering his greatest gift to his brothers. No, it is not a matter of being selfish or of running away from your responsibilities, but of contributing the MOST you have to offer to a world which desperately needs your help.

This must be a definite commitment and it is, indeed, a worthy one.

225. TO SEEK IS TO ASK FOR CHANGE

We know you desire to learn the TRUTH. You believe that knowing the TRUTH will save you much "time" and unnecessary pain – and it will.

In your pursuit, you will bring many of your old concepts into question and you will be shown that which does not fit the WORLD'S view of Reality. You have asked repeatedly to know how things really are and to have the blinders removed.

You knew, of course, this would lead you in a different direction – as it has.

To ask to know the TRUTH is to ask for change. It is a less traveled path and will lead you to experience many things which are out of kin with the majority of travelers. You must be strong enough to be able to "see" what is coming into sight.

You are still feeling the sting of the ancient curse placed upon those who dared go astray. The old path has been very carefully guarded to prevent any from departing from the "old way". When you began to realize that what you were seeing did not relate to what you were being told, this change began to creep into your direction. This is exactly what is now being experienced and it is more pronounced than you might think. Some are very conscious of these feelings, but others are only aware of a vague dissatisfaction with what they are experiencing. A new truth is definitely emerging, and it will claim its victory.

Those who are within the "fold" never have the courage of conviction to allow them to proceed with unfaltering steps in order to reach the new goal. As the image of the old system becomes more distorted, the number of fellow travelers will greatly increase. Do not allow the cries and threats of the PAST to retard your progress or to bring you to a halt. TRUTH will always continue to rise.

226. BUT YOU HAVE GROWN

Let us suppose that your present understanding and belief system suddenly reverted to that which it was some twenty years ago. Would you consider it to be a loss or a gain?

Actually...there is little question that generally speaking, most of you would find it to be quite a LOSS. Regardless of your "trials and tribulations", you as a conscious being have grown and benefited considerably from your experiences. Even though you may not wish to repeat many of them.

This is to say that you ARE aware of your inner growth and the wisdom you have achieved. In the course of a lifetime, your attainments are usually considerable – your progress can sometimes be remarkable indeed, and when your daily experiences are approached with this attitude, life becomes so much more interesting and meaningful for there is so very much to be gained. It is YOU however, who actually invites the experiences you encounter into your life. You are always free to choose them AND to make them what you wish.

It is by no means more noble or Spiritual to be unhappy or disillusioned than it is to experience a truly happy existence. The only validity is that which YOU give it.

We urge you to open your doors and windows and let the LIGHT of creation flow into your life. You have only to gain. In doing so, your contribution to others as well as to your world will become significant. The life process, (in itself), is indifferent and functions regardless of your approach, but you begin to LIVE when you make the decision to do so. Whether you see it or not, you are ALWAYS the captain of your voyage-there IS no other. May you always choose to go in God's Great Peace and Love. ALL IS ONE.

227. ON THE HORIZON

And signs of the approaching autumn are beginning to announce themselves while on the distant horizon, the energies of a new year are being formed by the IMAGES projected by the mind of man.

If you could but realize the power of your thoughts, you would make every effort to contribute your best...for in a very short while, it will no longer be possible to regress to this point to redirect your course.

You will be consigned to move forward from where you will then find yourselves. Your only power lies in this MOMENT.

How important it is to turn thoughts of hatred, distrust and revenge to those which you truly desire to experience. It is the ONLY solution to the problems you are now creating. It avails you nothing to PROJECT your responsibilities onto others, for they are in the same situation as are you. Do your mistaken concepts of your Creator REALLY mean so much to you that without bothering yourselves to EXAMINE them closely, you are willing to pay such a price?

Your Creator is far, far different from what you have been led to believe. You are each ITS dearly beloved child and your theologies can never change this. But your understanding can and indeed MUST change to include your brother – whoever he may be.

When this happens, you will behold your God EVERYWHERE you look, and you will find that you are already in paradise. GOD IS ALL THAT IS – ALL IS ONE.

Go in God's Great Peace and Love.

228. SEEK TO KNOW HIS WILL

Seek first to know HIS will and you will be shown.

It is to your greatest advantage to do so, especially before making a major decision, for there are always many more involved than you are aware.

Each of your actions touches others of whom you have little or no knowledge, for such is the nature of a holographic universe where all is truly ONE.

Even an apparently insignificant choice always has a bearing on your course throughout life.

When you come to abide in the consciousness of ONE, you will experience a complete transformation and your old world of chaos and fear will give birth to a new life of incredible LIGHT, LIFE and LOVE.

Regardless of how isolated you believe yourself to be, you are never alone, but are always in the MIDST of many who know and love you deeply.

Each of your decisions affects them also. Everything is connected – it is all ONE. When you do it unto the least of them, you do it unto The Christ also. When you seek first to know Christ's will, you WILL be shown.

PART XVII
THE LIGHT

229. THE STAR OF THE EAST

Once again, another year draws to its close and another chapter is added to the book in the great Hall of Records.

The drama of the world continues to repeat the habitual patterns of the past with ever greater intensity. Even so, there has been a turning point, for the Christ LIGHT is appearing increasingly all over the world.

From our perspective, it is awesome beyond words.

You too, will come to behold it with ever greater clarity, for it is growing so very swiftly. Rejoice that the time has come and that you are here.

Take every opportunity to point it out to others. It will only continue to grow in its brilliance. An entirely new reality is forming before your very eyes; make it yours, also.

MAKE IT YOURS!

Open yourselves to it in every possible way, for the LIGHT of a wondrous star is beginning to appear in the heavens and the actual manifestation of a cosmic legend is coming to pass.

The eternal Christ is claiming ITS own and gathering them from the four corners of the earth. The prophecy is now being fulfilled.

230. THE DAWN

To behold the LIGHT, you must look where the clouds are beginning to part. It is THERE and it will soon begin to break through.

With the passing of each day, the shadows grow dimmer and the veil of separation more ephemeral. You must patiently await that moment when the sun will, indeed, BURST through in all its splendor and the vague images of the Spiritual world will then glow in the REALITY of their being.

You will not find the LIGHT in the darkness of night nor behold the approaching dawn by searching the dark clouds.

Those who have been ANTICIPATING the dawn will be the first to behold its glorious rays. There are many who do not realize, as yet, that the night is ending but are trying to begin a new day in complete darkness.

They are stumbling about but getting nowhere. But you whose sleep has been restless and have been long awake do not see how you could BRIGHTEN their way. Offer them at least a candle that they do not slip and fall – but you could offer so much more by sharing YOUR Light with others.

Let your Light so shine that they, too, may see and glorify the Son that will be visible everywhere. Go forth in the LIGHT of the SON.

231. THE WAY OF THE ONE

THE WAY OF THE ONE is the way of LIGHT. His LIGHT shines upon you and permeates all of creation and none are denied it.

His Truth is contained within this LIGHT and all are bathed and sustained within its power. It exists from the beginning and has never diminished, for it is the source of all.

Nothing exists apart from this LIGHT.

What you see as darkness makes the LIGHT visible to man, for in its FULL brilliance, all becomes ONE.

Then, fear not the shadows, for they only give form and meaning to the LIGHT which would otherwise be overpowering.

The shadows are most visible where the LIGHT is most brilliant – they distinguish His truth. Allow, then, your sight to become ACCUSTOMED to this LIGHT and as the shadows recede, you will come to know that LIGHT IS ALL THAT IS and ALL IS, in truth, ONE.

Let your LIGHT, too, shine within THE ONE.

232. THE LIGHT

The LIGHT of the CONSCIOUSNESS of each will light his way and bring him unerringly to his goal.

This LIGHT, however, is but ONE, though it is refracted by each facet which receives it giving it the hue and radiance determined by each.

This LIGHT, then, is the manifestation of all possible colors, hues and intensities in their most brilliant and PURE form. Though all is in the process of Eternal change and becoming, it will always remain ONE. Each aspect completes the whole and is essential to its being.

This LIGHT is never diminished by the sending forth of its particles and waves, but simply continues to expand and radiate. It is continuous creation – ever expanding, ever becoming and moving forth.

Each hue, each intensity and refraction is essential to and included within the whole.

Let YOUR Light, then, so shine that all may rejoice in your contribution and proclaim the brilliance of THE ONE.

And God Said, "Let there be light"
And there was light.

Judaism

233. THE NEW COVENANT

The whole is contained in the most minute aspect of creation and this form is then repeated endlessly throughout the universe and on into INFINITY.

This pattern becomes the BUILDING BLOCK OF CREATION. IT IS LIGHT. IT IS ALL POWERFUL, ALL KNOWING AND EVERYWHERE PRESENT. It is LIGHT.

We have been showing how Light exists on many levels, dimensions and frequencies throughout Creation. It functions both within and beyond time. These building blocks are INFINITE, EQUAL AND ETERNAL. Everything is related. It is all creative and IT IS ALL ONE. There is NOTHING apart from IT, for it is ALL THAT IS.

Any division, any separation is illusion and you must come to realize this, to accept it and to begin to apply this understanding in your lives, for this is the TRUTH you are seeking and ONLY this will provide the answer. When you completely grasp this concept, your life will begin to take on new dimensions of which you had no hint whatsoever. This will usher in a new age unlike any the world has seen before. There will remain no arbitrary borders and boundaries, for all will know and understand.

It is already written on their hearts and all will come to know that this is the time awaited. What was whispered in the dark will soon be proclaimed from the housetops and it will appear at every hand and will be known by old and young alike. All will know it is GOD'S WORD. Rejoice that you are living at this time. You are to behold Creation in all its glory. Abide in Peace and Love.

He was in the beginning with God;
All things were made through Him,
And without Him

234. IT IS A HOLOGRAM

All of creation is HOLOGRAPHIC, for the whole is contained within its smallest building block. There is NO separation as you see it – ALL IS in the deepest sense, ONE.

The idea of separation exists only within the mind of man. There NEVER was a "fall" except from mans' awareness. GOD'S ONLY SON IS MANKIND... itself.

Each individual carries imprinted WITHIN, the image or matrix of the perfect man – THE CHRIST, which is a mirror, or perfect reflection of God, and each is destined to come to this awareness through the process of the Creator experiencing ITS OWN Creation THROUGH each. Each one is an EXTENSION of GOD.

Every aspect of creation will be experienced by His Only Son – the TOTALITY OF MANKIND – COMBINED.

He is IMMORTAL and He is ETERNAL.

There IS no death, for it is no more than the passing of a day... in eternity. The journey of each soul is unique – no two are, or CAN be the same.

There IS no one TRUTH apart from ONE. REJOICE IN YOUR UNIQUENESS – your CREATOR does!

It is ITS gift to you. Go forth, then, in God's Great Peace and Love. ALL IS ONE. GOD IS LOVE.

235. AND HE KNOWS EACH BY NAME

Your true name was known BEFORE the beginning. When the CREATOR divided ITSELF, you were already known and loved.

By NO means was your first appearance in the world on the day you were born into your present life. You have, indeed, had MANY names and faces since appearance as a SOUL, but you are always recognized by your TRUE name.

Your Spiritual IDENTITY has never changed apart from the CREATOR ITSELF, for you are ONE. YOU ARE THE PHYSICAL REFLECTION OF THE ONE, and every particle of your being is LIGHT.

This was the first act of creation. It is ETERNAL and it is known as THE CHRIST! In the course of the CREATOR experiencing ITS Creation through YOU, you will eventually come to REALIZE who you are – but THIS you have been since the beginning.

This period is the time of the Great Awakening and the CHRIST is being seen all over the world. His LIGHT will be seen by all, and for many, the Father and the Son will become ONE. This is occurring now. You are living in remarkable times. You are greatly blessed to be here.

Again, Jesus spoke to them saying,
"I am the Light of the world;
He who follows me will not walk in
darkness,
But will have the Light of life".

236. THE FESTIVAL OF LIGHTS

And one by one their Lights will begin to appear in every corner of the earth and their numbers will continue to increase as the time draws nigh.

Their Light shall be seen by all and all will know it is the Christ. Open your eyes and your hearts that He may enter.

He knows no race or creed, but only LOVE – and it will enter ever so gently where it is invited.

Welcome Him in WHATEVER form He appears, for He has many faces and vestments. His LIGHT will be unmistakable, and it is now appearing among you everywhere.

His word is love and His world is ONE which knows but PEACE and LOVE. Rejoice that you are living now, for you have been greatly blessed. Each will be called.

How will you answer?

237. I AM THE LIGHT

I am the LIGHT which shines within you and I am the LIGHT which shows your way. I am the LIGHT which illuminates your world and also the LIGHT of creation.

My LIGHT is Eternal and shines equally upon all, and so shall your LIGHT also. The LIGHT of my love bathes and warms everything in its radiance. Nothing is denied my love and my blessing. You are all the offspring of my love and my LIGHT shall guide you through eternity. If you, truly seek me, you will find me everywhere. I am never hidden from you for my radiance shines forth in all of creation.

You will find me in the smallest of creatures and in the poor and lowly as well as in the great. Each has a special place in my being and each of you is equally important to me, for I would be incomplete without a single one of you.

We are ONE and we are ALL THAT IS. It is all Sacred.

You never trod, but on sacred ground, and I impatiently await the day when each of you will finally gaze out upon creation and behold what I see. Your wonder and amazement will be my greatest joy and we will rejoice in our journey.

Your most bitter enemy will stand before you in such splendor and radiance as you have never beheld. You have much, so very much to look forward to and it saddens me that you have chosen to suffer as you do. You could behold this glory at any time you so desire, for it is already there and is patiently awaiting your awakening. There will not be one who will NOT experience this victory, for it has already been won. You will continue to hear my still small voice WITHIN you softly reminding you of who you are. Before you can see this in your brother, you must see it in Yourself!

238. TWO SHORT PRAYERS

Your Reality is also mine,
   For you are my SOURCE.
   I am Your expression in the physical world
   And I accept Your will as mine.
   I have naught to fear
   For we are Eternal, and we are ONE.

   GOD of my heart,
   Know that I am Yours.
   Be my constant guide in all things
   And I know I have naught to fear.
   Hasten to deliver us
   And bring us safely home. AMEN.

239. COUNT NO DAY LOST

Count no day lost
  If you have reached out
  To the One who created the stars
  And guides them on their paths,
  And warms the earth
  with the light of His countenance,
  For His love will guide you
  Unerringly along your way,
  And bring you safely home at last.
  Continue your journey
  In God.

240. BE STILL AND KNOW

Be still and know that I am God.

I am not distant and removed from you, but I dwell within every cell of your being.

Seek me also in the hills beyond.

For yes, I am there.

Seek me in the meadows and on the plain, I am there, too.

Wherever you go, you will find me -if you but know that I am there.

Yes, I too dwell within your world and I know it well, for I formed it from my own being.

It is beautiful and sacred to me.

As it is to some of you.

I am in each grain of sand – in every cloud.

The tears of my joy and sadness-water and nourish your forests and crops; I am always there.

Why then do you turn away-from the works of my hand?

Yet seldom fail to see my counterpart who, in truth, does not exist?

Why do you attempt to see other than what I have created for your own joy and growth?

The least of my creations is magnificent in my sight.

And I formed it with my deepest love and care.

Rejoice in the beauty that surrounds you, it is alive with the rhythm of my pulse and sustained by the breath of my love.

Seek where you will -you will find me where you seek...

And within your brother, as well.

241. BEGIN TO LIVE IT NOW

It would be highly beneficial to allow yourself each morning to enter into the new life you desire to experience.

Make every effort to assume the outlook and attitudes you would expect to have and begin to make them yours in every sense. Convince yourself that you are already living this new life and are now completely free of the bonds of the past. Approach everyone and every situation as a totally new opportunity with unlimited possibilities.

Remove the lenses – the filters of judgment and criticism from your eyes and look out on a new and pristine world – alive and vibrating with creative possibilities and eagerly waiting to respond to your deepest longings.

Accept nothing which is divisive and limiting and begin to assume your new role to the greatest extent possible for you.

If you are sincere in your efforts, you may find it far easier than you would have imagined for if you have been thinking along these lines, you will indeed have entered into this world.

Each success you have will further increase and strengthen your growth and you may be quite amazed at your progress. Your efforts along this line will also benefit others around you – some of whom you are not even aware.

This growth, however, will not be imaginary, but will be real in every sense. Claim it and make it yours and you will soon be well along your path. Go in God's Great Peace and Love.

242. BUT IT WASN'T REALITY

Softly the LIGHT spreads over the countryside and another day is dawning.

Mans' awakening from his sleep is releasing him from the nightmare HE has created and many there are who are realizing it wasn't reality.

The CONSCIOUS EVOLUTION is the TRUE one and it is growing swiftly.

It is very important to withhold judgment, for you cannot see the entire picture. Know that this truly is the end of an age and a new order is being called forth.

It is best to pass through these times as a CONSCIOUS OBSERVER, and to also offer encouragement to each. You are all far more closely related than you are yet aware.

Allow all fear to pass away along with the rest of the past, for it will NOT serve you.

Bring everything that you think, say and do to reflect Love for your brother, and it will be so. Release any you have consigned to hell and watch the response.

Go forth in God's Great Peace and Love. ALL IS WELL.

243. DREAMS

In a sense, dreams are the inner language of the soul.

They communicate information and ideas to you which concern your present life as well as outside circumstances. Dreams are important to your well-being and understanding and though you frequently do not recall them, they nevertheless fulfill their purpose on other levels. Those that you DO recall often call your attention to particular issues or situations in your life which need deeper consideration. In other words, they provide 'food for thought'.

As we have said, the dream world is no less real than is your daily life. One is as SUBSTANTIAL as the other and they are both formed in the same manner. Although you may not realize it, you often find yourselves in the same settings and with others there who are quite well known to you, but who may be complete strangers on this level. You also, as you well know, encounter others from your daily life as well as some who have gone on.

The dream world does not follow the laws which limit your daily lives. Dreams can also introduce that which is to come and help to prepare the way. They are often given as hints or clues and are significant to you.

Many times, you do not realize that a situation originated in a dream, for its appearance in your life seemed so natural and normal. It is not our intention to go deeply into the meanings of dreams which, as are your daily lives, highly individual in their meanings. The dream-world is unique, but it also revolves around YOU. It is a good practice to record your dreams and to review them from time to time.

If you are open to them, you will begin to find patterns and meanings within.

244. A PERFECT CHILD OF GOD

We must tell you once again – JUDGE no man, for you have no idea of whom you are speaking.

Those you might consider to be least worthy are PERFECT in the eyes of God.

You NEVER know with whom you are speaking and often your thoughts alone convey so much more than your words ever could.

Approach everyone you see as a PERFECT CHILD OF GOD – for this he IS. You must open your eyes to this TRUTH, for it will change your very being. The Christ comes to YOUR door, but YOU must open it. He knows YOU, but you seldom recognize HIM, for you are expecting someone quite different.

He has many faces, though if you could recognize but one, you would soon begin to see them all. He IS among you and you can most definitely expect to hear His knock.

His appearance will be DISTINCT for each of you.

Though His words will be the same, you will each hear them DIFFERENTLY. Open your heart to those around you...you have absolutely nothing to fear. It will never be a stranger who enters, but ANOTHER child of God.

You ARE being called, for He knows your name. Be prepared to receive Him. He WILL come to you. The time is NOW.

245. ACCEPT EACH DAY

Each day will open as the bud of a rare rose, and each will present a different picture, just as the beautiful flower.

Do not mourn, because they so quickly fade away, but rejoice, for there will always be another.

Accept that which each has to offer with joy and a grateful heart, for they are God's gift to you. Each is unique in ways which are at times difficult to distinguish, but each bears the mark of its Creator.

Each is telling you to do the same with each day which YOU are granted, for this is YOUR gift to Him who rejoices at the unique character and beauty of EACH of your days – regardless of how they may appear to you.

Continue each day in His Great Peace and Love. ALL IS AS IT MUST BE.

246. AWAKENING FROM THE DREAM

How softly the morning dawns on a sleeping world and the golden rays of the morning sun begin to dance through the leaves and the grass.

The TRUTH of Creation likewise begins to dawn upon a sleeping world and the shadows of the darkness begin to fade and give way to the brilliance of the sun. The night has been long, and mans' eyes are still unaccustomed to the brightness, but the time will be short before the full LIGHT of day covers the countryside. It will be as the awakening from a dream which has distorted your vision and given you a strange and unreal view of life. You must now begin to cast aside all that has been confusing and unreal and to gaze upon the world as it now begins to appear in the full Light of day.

For some, the dreams of the night were as nightmares filled with terrors and demons. For others, there were periods of confusion and questions. Some were in a dream which seemed to be pleasant, though vague and unclear. Such will be your memories of THIS world.

As the Light becomes stronger and clearer, you will begin to see how distorted your view has been. You will rejoice in the clarity and beauty which will surround you and the old doubts and fears will quickly disappear. You have much to look forward to and you will be completely overcome by the peace and beauty which will surround you. The love and joy which you will find everywhere will be beyond description and soon, your memories of the dream will fade quietly away. You will be left with only the TRUTHS which you managed to discover in your past dream.

They will remain as your treasure which you so painfully managed to extract from the confusion. You will bask in the unity of your new world and you will fully realize that ALL IS ONE!

Your Spiritual Path
Is the Creator
Experiencing all It created
Through THE CHRIST.
THE FATHER AND SON ARE ONE:
LIGHT, LIFE AND LOVE –
FATHER, SON AND HOLY SPIRIT,
SACRED, INFINITE AND ETERNAL.
IT IS ALL THAT IS.
Your Spiritual Path
Is the Creator
Experiencing all It created
Through THE CHRIST.
The Father and Son are ONE:
LIGHT, LIFE and LOVE –
FATHER, SON and HOLY SPIRIT SACRED, INFINITE and
ETERNAL.
IT IS ALL THAT IS.